The Official Cookbook of Critical Role

EXQUISITE EXANDRIA

LIZ MARSHAM

WITH RECIPES BY

Jesse Szewczyk, Susan Vu & Amanda Yee

FOREWORD BY

QUYEN TRAN & SAM RIEGEL

Random House Worlds
NEW YORK

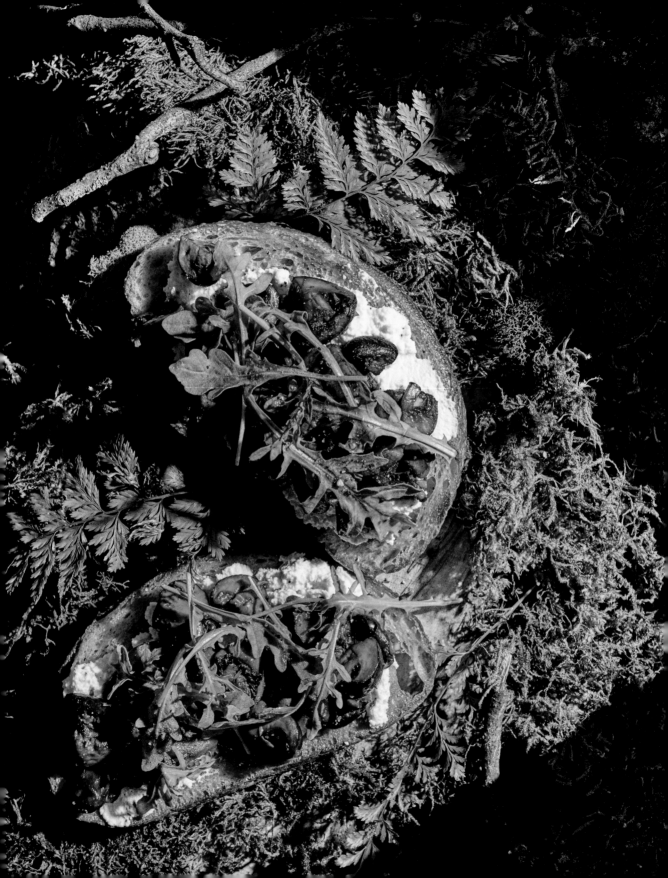

Contents

foreword

by Quyen Tran and Sam Riegel

QUYEN TRAN: Most fans of *Critical Role* love it for the cast's fantastic characters, Matt's thrilling plot, and the intricate lore and world building. But for me—it's all about the FOOD. Yes, the cuisine of Exandria defines the atmosphere for the audience in a way that—

SAM RIEGEL: Hold on. Stop. What is going on here?

QT: Oh, hi hon. I'm writing the foreword to *Exquisite Exandria*—your company's new cookbook featuring yummy dishes and mouth-watering tastes inspired by all three Critical Role campaigns.

SR: But . . . why did they ask you? Why not me? I'm one of the founders of Critical Role! I'm Sam Riegel!

QT: <SIGH> Because, Sam, I'm not only your wife. I've also been a lifelong baker, whose charity project "Dough-rectors of Photography" raised thousands of dollars for charities, like the LA Regional Food Bank and Vote Save America, during the pandemic. Or maybe because I've been cooking my entire life, whipping up tremendously complex dishes to feed our family while you sit on the couch dreaming up silly ads for your internet show.

SR: Yeah. I guess that makes sense. But what if I have something insightful to say about this book?

QT: Do you . . . ?

SR: Carry on, my love.

QT: As I was saying . . . for me, the coolest part of Exandria is the level of detail Matt puts into describing the flavors and smells of the cuisine—the succulent offerings of Marquet bazaars, the prim and proper table menu of Whitestone banquets, the sumptuous delights of the far reaches of Wildemount. It's a level of detail that you don't find in many adventure stories. The food that one encounters traveling across Exandria doesn't just help immerse the audience into the story, it makes us downright HUNGRY. And this wonderfully crafted cookbook is a remarkable chance to share the wonders of Matt's imaginary cuisine and make it a tastable, cookable reality. The chefs, cooks, tasters, editors, writers, artists, and photographers who contributed to this book poured themselves into developing recipes that aren't merely homages to their favorite fantasy campaign—they're actually really great dishes. And armed with the recipes in these pages, you'll be able to entertain guests with novel, and sometimes very strange, dinners, while sharing the stories of Critical Role to a new, hungry audience.

SR: Wow. The way you describe it, it makes me excited to learn some recipes and get my hands dirty in the kitchen!

QT: Oh? Does that mean you're going to actually help me cook dinner tonight?

SR: Well, I mean. I've got this new cat costume I need to try on. It's for a commercial skit we're doing this week so—

QT: Don't worry about it, hon. I'll handle the cooking—and the foreword. You just go do . . . whatever it is you do.

SR: Thanks, babe. You're the best.

QT: And for the rest of you, get out your whisks. Put on your aprons. And get ready to prepare some wild, wonderful, too-good-to-be-real dishes!

Introduction

It began, as the best things do, with a group of friends sitting around a table.

We were reading *The Daring Trials and Tribulations of Sir Taryon Darrington* in our book club. (If you haven't read it yourself, give it a try: it is a wild ride.) Since most of us are good with food, and a book club is hardly worth the name without snacks, we try to bring treats themed to the book we're reading. Sir Darrington does provide quite a bit of detail about everything in his adventures, including what he eats. Some of his accounts were confounding, though. For instance, a drink called Changebringer's Nectar that he describes as "maple syrup grain alcohol" sounds terrible, but he declares it to be tasty. We were intrigued.

As we mentioned, most of us are skilled at experimenting with food and having it come out well. (One of us, it must be said, is hopeless in the kitchen. She's great at complimenting the chefs, though, and she spins a good yarn.) But we found that Sir Darrington's descriptions, while evocative, weren't enough to actually cook from. We needed more information. How does one actually *make* this stuff?

Happily, one of us was traveling through Deastok soon after that, and she managed to talk the bartender at the Grumpy Lily tavern into giving up *two* of his recipes. He may have been willing to share his secrets because both drinks are nearly impossible to make at home, but we were undeterred. We tried. We failed. We tried again. Finally, we reproduced versions of both drinks that we were satisfied with, and we celebrated by drinking far too much of them.

We had triumphed, and we wanted to do it again. Now it was bothering us: there were so many special meals, so many delicious drinks, throughout Exandria that we had never tried, never mind tried to make. We wanted more exploration, more experimentation, more recipes. We aren't cut out to be brigadiers like Taryon and his crew, but we could have adventures in our own way. We could find our own type of treasure. It turned into a hobby: go on vacation, bring back a recipe. Then it turned into a mission: who can get to Vasselheim in time for Highsummer?

In our search for food, we found far more stories than we were expecting. It turns out the two are tied together more often than not, and the food is so much better when you know how it came to be. So we collected recipes, and we collected tales, and we brought them back to share with one another around the table. Before we knew it, our book club had created a book. There is so much more to explore and eat and make in this world, but it became time for us to stop sharing with one another and start sharing with you.

Here, at last, is the product of our adventures, a list of our labors, little slices of this exquisite place we live in that you can re-create at home. We hope you enjoy these banquets, bites, and beverages from across Exandria—and the stories behind them.

—The *Exquisite Exandria* creators, formerly the First Draught Book Club

I
TAL'DOREI

TAL'DOREI

You may think you know what Tal'Dorei cuisine is like. *Oh*, you say, *I've eaten at A Taste of Tal'Dorei. I've had Thordak's Pepper Poppers; it's basically like I've been to Emon. Why, the Rimelord told me I might survive his frozen death!*

Or perhaps, reading this, you're forming a different impression. *Ah, you're thinking. They're about to dunk hard on A Taste of Tal'Dorei. Here it comes! Make sure to mention the bored theater majors pretending they're evil warlords and stuff!*

So let's get this out of the way, right at the beginning: if there is a place in Exandria today that has earned its cheesy enjoyments, it's Tal'Dorei. If there is a place worthy of celebrating with overblown drama and collectible pencils, it's Tal'Dorei. Come with us on a short tour of the past, so we can remind you of the forces shaping Tal'Dorei's culture, cuisine, and dinner theater entertainment alike. Because, while all

of Exandria has been through turmoil, Tal'Dorei is the place that has been most recently and thoroughly turned upside down.

No corner of Exandria, of course, escaped the ravages of the Calamity. Afterward, the land that would become Tal'Dorei went through a time of rebuilding. The dwarves beneath the northern mountains burrowed deep to form the subterranean city of Kraghammer. A group of elves who had magically transported themselves to the Fey Realm to escape the terrors of the Calamity returned to the Verdant Expanse in the south, founding the city of Syngorn. Then humans crossed the Ozmit Sea and spread up the western side of Tal'Dorei, establishing settlements and fighting for power.

Eventually the humans' shortsightedness and violence erupted into war. Three decades of bloodshed and tumult later, a young warrior named Zan Tal'Dorei reunified people under her leadership. A council was nominated to rule alongside her in the capital city of Emon. The realm was renamed in her honor. Everyone was ready to lay down their arms and rest.

But, just two years later, Errevon the Rimelord attacked the still-reeling continent. The Tal'Dorei Council, Syngorn, and Kraghammer united against the ice elemental spirit, pushed him back into the rift, and with the help of the Ashari druids, sealed it.

The land had been permanently altered. Two formerly fertile regions were cursed and scarred by the wars, known ever after as the blighted Umbra Hills and the icy Frostweald. Finally, though, a period of peace came. Tal'Dorei became an empire. Generations passed. The upheavals in the land were minor and absorbed with relative aplomb. When

a wizard living in the Bramblewood botched a spell and flooded the eastern forest with a thousand surprised chickens, the enterprising folks of nearby Westruun just shrugged and set up a new export market. The Great Feathering of 641 PD is still spoken of in mostly fond terms, a minor blip in a calm century. Still, in hindsight, it doesn't seem like enough rest.

About fifty years ago, the avaricious red dragon known as Thordak, the Cinder King, laid waste to the Mornset Countryside in the south. His banishment to the Elemental Plane of Fire lasted more than a decade, but while there, he grew stronger and formed an alliance with four other chromatic dragons. At the end of 810 PD, Thordak broke free of his planar prison, and the Chroma Conclave ravaged Emon. Thordak settled amid the ruins of the capital, while his three compatriots spread out across the continent, bringing devastation wherever their attention landed.

And by then he only had three remaining compatriots, because the adventuring group Vox Machina had already dispatched the blue dragon Brimscythe.

Eventually all the land would hear of these heroes: Vax'ildan, the thief and assassin from Byroden who became the champion of the Matron of Ravens, goddess of death. Vex'ahlia, Vax's twin sister, the broomstick-riding archer who became the champion of the Dawnfather, and her bear companion, Trinket. Percival Fredrickstein von Musel Klossowski de Rolo III, lord of Whitestone and Vex's eventual husband, the deadly marksman and brilliant inventor who built Exandria's first firearms. Keyleth of the Air Ashari, wielder of nature magic, who became the near-immortal Voice of the Tempest. Grog Strongjaw, the hulking half-giant brawler, who

forged the weapons that defeated a god. Scanlan Shorthalt, teller of tales, singer of sorcerous songs, and master of the magical mansion, who became the champion of the Knowing Mentor. And Pike Trickfoot, warrior and healer of the Everlight, who brought most of the group back from the dead, some of them multiple times.*

Together, wielding force, diplomacy, leadership, and a set of truly legendary arms and armor, Vox Machina slew the remaining four dragons of the Chroma Conclave. It took them only four weeks.

But in those weeks, so much damage had been done. Countless people were dead, thousands of acres of crops were destroyed, supply routes and food stores across the continent were strained to their breaking point. The stability and structure of Tal'Dorei had been turned on its head. Again.

And now, today, is a time of rebuilding in Tal'Dorei. Again. Many find themselves focusing inward, away from

Taryon Darrington, the arcane builder and author from Wildemount and original spark of inspiration for this book, joined the group after their defeat of the Chroma Conclave. He left a short time later to form the heralded Darrington Brigade.

the wider world. The year after Thordak and his allies were slain, news arrived: Vox Machina was confronting a lich who threatened the existence of everyone in Exandria. *Where is this lich?* the people of Tal'Dorei asked. *Across the sea, in Issylra,* came the answer. *Well, then,* people responded, *we'll worry about that trouble when it gets here.* Since then, a generation of relative quiet has come and gone, but Tal'Dorei has not had nearly enough rest.

This, finally, brings us to the food of Tal'Dorei today, and we are honored to bring you the recipes that follow. From Whitestone in the north to the Rifenmist Jungle in the south, we have gathered dishes of every size, from a quick snack to a breakfast feast. Tal'Dorei's grand institution of greasy pub food is of course represented. The bounty of Tal'Dorei's lush forests is referenced with several instances of tree nuts, though we have limited ourselves to the common varieties and would not recommend delving into the Verdant Expanse in search of fey-touched food. Even the Great Feathering gets a nod, as we feature chicken in several of our selections (though poultry has also

become trendy on the continent in recent decades, after word spread that Scanlan Shorthalt was partial to it).

But those are just ingredients, and what ties Tal'Dorei cuisine together is more a matter of culture. For that, let's return to contemplating everyone's favorite historically themed dinner theater. Because A Taste of Tal'Dorei, when you get down to it, understands the continent it is celebrating.

Amid the spectacle and the breading, the thing that A Taste of Tal'Dorei gets most right is the emphasis on comfort. *Enjoy your drinks. Pack in the food. It's been hard out there, and it will be hard again. The rest will never last long enough, not nearly. But in here, while we're eating, it's okay. Hoist that souvenir tankard high. We will all survive the Rimelord's frozen death.*

And so, we invite you to make these meals in the same spirit. Whether it's pastries or pies, meat or mayonnaise, we hope these dishes can bring you a moment of respite in a rough world, a taste of Tal'Dorei in a troubled time. Cheers.

Slayer's Cake

After halting an evil god's incursion into the Lightless Lands Below, joining the Vasselheim hunting guild the Slayer's Take, liberating the city of Whitestone from the rule of Delilah and Sylas Briarwood, defeating five dragons, and along the way, resurrecting their party members from death ten separate times, the heroes of Vox Machina needed a break from adventuring. But they found that they couldn't sit idle. So half of the team—Vex'ahlia, Pike, Keyleth, and Taryon—decided to use their skills at hunting fearsome beasts, channeling the divine, harnessing the elements, and building robots to . . . open a bakery. The result was the Slayer's Cake in Whitestone!

The bakery's opening seasons were somewhat bumpy,* but the renown of its founders and the ongoing refinements to their recipes paid off. The Slayer's Cake is now loved across Tal'Dorei and beyond. Even though the bakery is branching out into new territories, access to its wares is still limited: if you can't get to Whitestone, Emon, or Nicodranas, you're out of luck.

Until now.

Here you will find the original, proprietary recipes for three of the Slayer's Cake's most notable delicacies. The spicy smoothness of Sun Treats. The tangy creaminess of Everlight-as-Air Scones. And, of course, the nutty deliciousness of Trinket's Bear Claws (with a cinnamon kick, if you prefer them Nicodranas-style). They can now be yours at any time, no adventuring required.

One notable bump: the time their new hire turned out to be a bounty hunter who promptly kidnapped Taryon.

recipe continues ☞

Everlight-as-Air Scones

PREP TIME: 35 minutes
COOK TIME: 20 minutes

1⅓ cups / 315ml heavy cream, cold, plus more for brushing on the scones

1½ teaspoons vanilla extract

2½ cups / 350g all-purpose flour, plus more for dusting

⅓ cup / 65g granulated sugar

2½ teaspoons baking powder

¾ teaspoon kosher salt

½ teaspoon ground ginger

⅓ cup / 55g finely chopped candied or crystallized ginger

1 tablespoon turbinado sugar

Papaya-Lemon Curd, for serving (recipe follows)

In a 2-cup / 475ml liquid measuring cup, whisk together the heavy cream and the vanilla extract. Chill in the refrigerator while the oven preheats.

Preheat the oven to 425°F / 220°C. Line a large baking sheet with parchment paper and set aside.

In a large bowl, whisk together the flour, granulated sugar, baking powder, salt, and ground ginger. Add the candied or crystallized ginger and use your hands to toss the ginger in the flour mixture until it is no longer sticky.

Drizzle one-third of the chilled heavy cream mixture over the dry ingredients, then gently toss and stir with your hands. Repeat this two additional times until all of the heavy cream has been added and the mixture has come together to form a shaggy dough. Use your hands to gently bring the dough together, but do not overwork the dough (a few dry patches in the dough is fine).

Lightly dust a clean work surface with flour, then top with the dough. Gently pat the dough into a ¾-inch-thick circle that is about 8 inches / 20cm across. Cut the dough into eight equal wedges. Separate the wedges and arrange on the prepared baking sheet. Refrigerate for 20 minutes.

Brush the tops and sides of the chilled scones with additional heavy cream and sprinkle with the turbinado sugar.

Bake until the scones are puffed and golden brown, about 20 minutes, rotating the baking sheet once after 10 minutes.

Transfer the scones to a cooling rack and cool for 10 minutes. Serve warm with Papaya-Lemon Curd on the side.

recipe and ingredients continue ☞

The full Emon

Mornings should never be faced on an empty stomach. But sometimes your standard breakfast fare just won't cut it—especially on a morning that follows a long night of celebration and indulgence. When battle is impending, diplomatic negotiation is imminent, or your head feels like it's about to implode, you need a serious food boost. This tasty spread, created by the Diamond Nest Tavern and adopted by pubs throughout Emon, has you covered:

Salt and grease craving? Load up on eggs and thick slab bacon.

Want something crispy? Try the chicken and the tomatoes, fried to perfection.

Need a pick-me-up? You've got one; the gravy is full of coffee.

Sweet tooth? Check out the waffles with lots of extras.

Hair of the dog? One of the extras in that waffle is beer.

Put the spring back in your step, settle your stomach, and prepare to face the far-too-bright day with the Full Emon.

recipe continues ☞

Sweet and Sticky Slab Bacon, Fried Tomatoes, and Fried Eggs

PREP TIME: 25 minutes
COOK TIME: 2 hours 50 minutes

____

2 cups / 475ml hard apple cider

¼ cup / 60ml honey, plus 2 tablespoons

1 tablespoon yellow mustard seeds

½ teaspoon crushed red pepper flakes

One 1½-pound / 680g piece slab bacon

Canola oil, for frying

11 eggs

Kosher salt and freshly ground black pepper

1 cup / 140g all-purpose flour

1 cup / 140g cornmeal

1 cup / 60g panko bread crumbs

1½ teaspoons granulated garlic

¾ teaspoon paprika

¼ teaspoon cayenne pepper

3 large, firm heirloom tomatoes, cut into ½-inch-thick slices (about 12 slices total)

Preheat the oven to 325°F / 165°C. In a 9 by 13-inch / 23 by 33cm baking dish, stir together the hard apple cider, ¼ cup / 60ml of the honey, the mustard seeds, and red pepper flakes. Add the slab bacon, skin side down, and turn to coat in the cooking liquid. Place the baking dish on a baking sheet, cover the dish with foil, and braise in the oven for 1 hour. Remove the baking dish from the oven, turn the bacon over, cover again with foil, and continue to braise until the bacon is tender, about 1 more hour. Remove from the oven and turn off the heat. Remove the foil and let the bacon cool completely in the liquid, about 2 hours.

Line a baking sheet with aluminum foil and set aside. Remove the bacon from the braising liquid and cut crosswise into ¼-inch-thick slices. Arrange the bacon slices on the prepared baking sheet in a single layer. Skim and discard the excess fat from the top of the braising liquid and transfer the remaining liquid (about 1½ cups / 360ml) to a medium saucepan. Bring to a boil over medium-high heat, then lower the heat to a strong simmer and cook until reduced to ½ cup / 120ml, 20 to 25 minutes. Pour the thin glaze into a small bowl and stir in the remaining 2 tablespoons of honey. Set aside while you preheat the oven; the glaze will thicken up slightly as it sits.

Preheat the oven to 425°F / 220°C. Brush the tops of the slab bacon with some of the glaze and bake until the glaze is bubbling and the bacon is lightly caramelized in spots, 7 to 10 minutes. Gently turn the bacon slices over, brush with more glaze, and cook until the second side is lightly browned and caramelized, 5 to 7 additional minutes. Brush any

recipe continues ☛

Line a small plate with paper towels and set aside. In a large saucepan over medium heat, cook the bacon, stirring occasionally, until the fat has rendered and the bacon is crispy, 10 to 14 minutes. Transfer to the prepared plate to absorb any excess fat and set aside. There should be about 3 tablespoons of bacon fat in the saucepan. If there is more, pour it off for another use.

Sprinkle the remaining 3½ tablespoons of flour over the bacon fat in the saucepan and cook, whisking constantly, for 2 minutes. Slowly pour in the chicken stock and remaining ½ cup / 120ml of coffee and cook, whisking constantly, until no lumps of flour remain. Continue to whisk until the mixture comes to a simmer, 6 to 8 minutes. Simmer, whisking occasionally, until the mixture is thickened and the consistency is a smooth and velvety gravy, 7 to 10 minutes. The gravy should coat a spoon nicely but will not be super thick at this point. This is ideal, since it will thicken up as it sits. Season to taste with salt and black pepper. Turn off the heat and cover with a lid to keep it warm while you fry the chicken.

Place a second wire rack on a second baking sheet and set aside. Add 4 of the dredged chicken drumsticks to the hot oil and fry, turning the pieces occasionally, until evenly golden brown and cooked through, 12 to 15 minutes. While the chicken cooks, adjust the heat as needed to maintain the oil temperature between 300°F and 325°F / 150°C and 165°C. Remove the drumsticks from the oil with a slotted spoon or tongs, set on the second wire rack, and season with additional salt. Bring the oil back to 350°F / 175°C and repeat with the remaining dredged chicken drumsticks.

Transfer the fried chicken to a large platter. Pour the gravy (reheated, if needed) into a gravy boat or serving bowl, scatter the crispy bacon on top, and serve immediately.

Malty Beer Waffles with Orange-Honey Browned Butter Syrup

PREP TIME: 20 minutes
COOK TIME: 25 minutes
SPECIAL EQUIPMENT: One 7-inch / 18cm round Belgian waffle iron

———

Zest and juice of 1 large orange (about 1 tablespoon zest and ¼ cup / 60ml juice)

3 tablespoons granulated sugar

1¼ cups / 175g all-purpose flour

½ cup / 70g cornstarch

Kosher salt

2 teaspoons baking powder

1¾ teaspoons baking soda

1 egg

1 egg white

⅔ cup / 160ml IPA beer, at room temperature

½ cup / 120ml milk, at room temperature

2 teaspoons vanilla extract

4 tablespoons / 55g unsalted butter, melted and cooled slightly

In a large bowl, place the orange zest and granulated sugar and use your fingers to rub the zest into the sugar. Add the flour, cornstarch, ¾ teaspoon of salt, and the baking powder and baking soda and whisk until well combined.

In a medium bowl, whisk together the egg and egg white until light and frothy. Add the IPA beer, milk, orange juice, and vanilla extract and whisk together until smooth. Whisk in the melted butter. Add the milk mixture to the flour mixture and whisk until just combined (do not overmix; some small lumps are okay). Allow to rest for 20 minutes.

WHILE THE BATTER RESTS, MAKE THE ORANGE-HONEY BROWNED BUTTER SYRUP: In a medium saucepan over medium heat, melt the butter, stirring frequently, until light brown specks start to form and the butter starts to smell nutty, 5 to 7 minutes. Remove from the heat and immediately whisk in the orange marmalade, honey, and salt. The mixture will seem separated at first, but keep whisking and it will come together to form a smooth, glossy sauce. Cover with a lid to keep warm while you make the waffles.

Preheat the oven to 200°F / 95°C and preheat a 7-inch / 18cm Belgian waffle iron to between medium and medium-high heat according to the manufacturer's directions. Place a cooling rack on a baking sheet and set aside.

Spray the hot waffle iron lightly with nonstick cooking spray and ladle one-quarter of the batter (about 1 scant cup / 240ml) onto the waffle iron. Close the top and cook until the waffle is cooked through, browned, and crispy, about 5 minutes. Transfer the cooked waffle to the cooling rack and place the baking sheet in the warm oven. Repeat the process

Orange-Honey Browned Butter Syrup

6 tablespoons / 85g unsalted butter

½ cup / 150g orange marmalade

¼ cup / 60ml honey

½ teaspoon kosher salt

½ cup / 60g chopped pecans, toasted

Whipped Cream

⅔ cup / 160ml heavy cream, cold

2 tablespoons confectioners' sugar

½ teaspoon vanilla extract

with the remaining batter to make 3 more waffles, adding the cooked waffles to the baking sheet to keep warm.

TO MAKE THE WHIPPED CREAM: In a large bowl, combine the heavy cream, confectioners' sugar, and vanilla extract. Use an electric handheld mixer on medium speed to whip until it forms medium-stiff peaks, 2 to 3 minutes.

To serve, rewarm the syrup ever so slightly over low heat, stirring constantly, until it loosens up and drizzles from a spoon easily (similar to caramel sauce or thick maple syrup). If needed, stir in a splash of water to reach that consistency. Stir in the toasted chopped pecans. Set each warm waffle on an individual plate, then top evenly with the syrup and dollops of the whipped cream. Serve immediately.

The Grand Poobah's GoFiBePo Meat Board

One blessed day in the town of Whitestone, Grog Strongjaw walked into the castle kitchen and requested "a salad with meat in it." Because Grog carried the title of Grand Poobah de Doink of All of This and That, the kitchen staff took his request with due seriousness but a lack of comprehension. Within an hour, they had created a salad with *only* meat in it, and the official dish of Whitestone* was born. Grog has declared that the resulting bowl of salted goat, fish, beef, and pork—dubbed GoFiBePo—must not be eaten with utensils. We here at Exquisite Exandria additionally declare that it must not be eaten at all, unless you have a constitution to match Grog's.** As a more palatable alternative, may we present this charcuterie board, which will feed a dozen people without giving them the worst meat sweats of their lives.

*Approval pending.
**This excludes most of the population of Exandria.

Serves 10 to 12

PREP TIME: 3 to 4 hours
COOK TIME: 1 hour 30 minutes

recipe continues ☞

Meats of fish, Spam hash, Goat, and Bacon

SMOKED FISH DIP

4 ounces / 115g smoked trout or smoked salmon fillets

½ cup / 125g cream cheese

¼ cup / 60g mayonnaise

¼ cup / 60g full-fat sour cream

3 tablespoons chopped fresh chives

3 tablespoons chopped fresh parsley

2 tablespoons Worcestershire sauce

1 tablespoon fusaka seasoning (page 134) or Old Bay seasoning

Zest and juice of 1 small lemon

Kosher salt and freshly ground black pepper

In a medium bowl, place the trout, cream cheese, mayonnaise, sour cream, chives, parsley, Worcestershire sauce, fusaka, and lemon zest and juice, and combine using an electric handheld mixer. Season with salt and pepper.

Transfer to a serving bowl and cover. Refrigerate for up to 24 hours before placing on a charcuterie board.

Pairs super well with cucumbers, sourdough, grapes, and Flatbread Crackers (page 46).

FRIED SPAM CUBES

Two 12-ounce / 340g cans Spam, cut into 1-inch / 2.5cm cubes

Heat a large pan over high heat. Once hot, lower to medium-high and fry the Spam cubes until golden brown on all sides, about 2 minutes for each side. Drain on a paper towel and skewer with appetizer toothpicks.

Try with Ale and Cheddar Fondue (page 44), Buttery Brioche Spears (page 46), apples, and pepper Jack cheese.

recipe and ingredients continue ↪

LAMB OR GOAT PÂTÉ

4 tablespoons / 55g butter

1 medium shallot, cut into
¼-inch dice

1 lamb or goat liver, cut
into 1-inch / 2.5cm cubes
(see Note)

Kosher salt and freshly
ground black pepper

2 tablespoons brandy

½ cup / 120ml heavy cream

1 tablespoon chopped
fresh thyme

POCKET BACON
(PAGE 156)

Heat a medium saucepan over medium heat. Once hot, add the butter and shallot. Sauté the shallot until aromatic, 2 to 3 minutes. Add the liver and stir. Season with salt and pepper. When the liver has cooked about 3 to 5 minutes, add in the brandy and continue cooking until the alcohol has evaporated, about 2 minutes. The liver should be fully cooked and reach a temperature of 145°F / 63°C.

Transfer the pan contents to a blender and add the cream and thyme. Blend until smooth. Season with salt and pepper.

Strain through a fine-mesh strainer into a standard-size ramekin or small serving bowl. Cover and refrigerate for up to 24 hours.

Try with Onion Jam (page 45), Comté cheese, cucumbers, grapes, and brioche spears (page 46) or sourdough.

NOTE: You may need to ask your local butcher several days in advance for a lamb or goat liver.

Fruit, Veggies, and Cheese

1 pint / 350g strawberries, washed, hulled, and halved

1 pound / 450g green or red seedless grapes, washed and cut into 5 or 6 clusters

2 large green apples, cored and cut into slices

1 large cucumber, cut into 3-inch / 7.5cm spears

20 small radishes, halved lengthwise

8 ounces / 225g Comté cheese, cut into ¼-inch-thick rectangles

8 ounces / 225g pepper Jack cheese, cut into ¼-inch-thick rectangles

ALE AND CHEDDAR FONDUE

16 ounces / 475 ml pale ale

2 tablespoons Worcestershire sauce

1 tablespoon garlic powder

1 tablespoon powdered mustard

1 tablespoon ground white pepper

3 cups / 384g shredded Cheddar cheese

2 tablespoons all-purpose flour

Kosher salt

In a medium pot over low heat, stir together the ale, Worcestershire sauce, garlic powder, mustard powder, and pepper until combined.

In a small bowl, toss the shredded Cheddar with the flour. Once incorporated, vigorously stir the cheese and flour into the ale mixture until the sauce is free of lumps, then continue to simmer for 10 to 12 minutes. Season with salt.

Lower the heat to the lowest setting and keep warm, stirring occasionally, until ready to serve.

Fondue pairs well with apples, grapes, Pickled Cauliflower (page 45), radishes, Fried Spam Cubes (Page 42), Pocket Bacon (page 156), and Flatbread Crackers or brioche spears (page 46).

recipe and ingredients continue ☞

Accoutrements

ONION JAM

¼ cup / 60ml olive oil

2 large sweet onions, sliced ¼ inch thick

1 cup / 200g granulated sugar

¾ cup / 175ml white wine vinegar

2 dried bay leaves

3 tablespoons fresh thyme leaves, finely chopped

1 teaspoon ground white pepper

Kosher salt

Heat a medium pan over medium heat. Add the oil and onions. Cook until golden brown, about 12 minutes, stirring occasionally.

When the onions are golden, sprinkle with the sugar, increase the heat to high, and stir until the sugar melts. Add the white wine vinegar, bay leaves, thyme, and white pepper. Simmer, stirring occasionally, until the liquid is reduced by half, 5 to 7 minutes.

The onion jam should be thick and semi-sticky. Transfer to a sterilized, sealable jar and refrigerate overnight.

To serve, place the onion jam in a small serving bowl and bring to room temperature before serving on a charcuterie board.

Pairs super well with pâté (see page 43), Comté cheese, pepper Jack cheese, cucumbers, grapes, sourdough, and Flatbread Crackers (page 46).

PICKLED CAULIFLOWER

1 medium cauliflower, broken into florets

1 tablespoon cumin seeds

1 tablespoon black peppercorns

2 garlic cloves, peeled

1 cup / 240ml pickling vinegar

½ cup / 120ml water

½ cup / 100g granulated sugar

2 tablespoons kosher salt

In a large sterilized, sealable jar, combine the cauliflower florets, cumin seeds, black peppercorns, and garlic cloves.

In a small pot over medium heat, combine the pickling vinegar, water, sugar, and salt. Simmer until reduced by a third, 10 to 15 minutes. Pour the liquid over the jar contents. Loosely cover the jar and let cool to room temperature before sealing. Refrigerate overnight.

Drain and serve in 1 or 2 small bowls on a charcuterie board.

Can be stored for up to 2 weeks in the fridge.

recipe and ingredients continue ☞

Grog's Garlicky Mayonnaise (also, fries)

After Vox Machina killed the dragon Umbrasyl, Grog found a rune-covered ceramic jug buried under Umbrasyl's hoarded gold. Strangely, the jug made sloshing noises even when empty. Grog did some experimenting* and discovered that it could make gallons of liquid on command. Ale, water, salt water, more ale. And mayonnaise, which he ate straight from the jar until it was gone. Grog is perfectly happy with this simple snack, but he has admitted** that it could be improved on by scooping up the mayo with something besides his fingers. We suggest these oven-roasted herbed fries. We've also included a way to fancy up your straight-from-the-jar mayonnaise, or should you not have access to a magic jug, make your own from scratch.

*Experiments included repeatedly shaking the jug, trying to break the jug, letting Percy and Keyleth fill the jug with dragon blood and dirt, and wearing the jug as a hat.

**Grudgingly.

PREP TIME: 20 minutes
COOK TIME: 1 hour

Oven Fries

1½ pounds / 680g russet potatoes (about 3 medium or 2 large potatoes)

⅓ cup / 80ml olive oil

1½ teaspoons finely minced fresh rosemary leaves (from about 1 large sprig; see Notes)

1 teaspoon kosher salt

½ teaspoon freshly ground black pepper

2 garlic cloves, minced

Grated Parmesan cheese, for serving (optional)

*T*O MAKE THE OVEN FRIES: Set a rack in the bottom third of the oven and preheat to 425°F / 220°C.

Scrub the potatoes under cold running water. Cut lengthwise into planks, ½ inch thick, then cut each plank into ½-inch-thick batons. Transfer the cut potatoes to a large mixing bowl. Add the olive oil and toss to evenly coat. Transfer to an unlined baking sheet along with any remaining olive oil left in the bowl. Spread the potatoes out in a single layer.

Roast, turning the potatoes halfway through baking with a thin metal spatula, until deep golden brown and crispy, 40 to 50 minutes total. Add the rosemary, salt, pepper, and garlic and carefully toss the fries to evenly coat them. Continue baking until the rosemary and garlic are fragrant, 4 to 6 minutes more. Remove from the oven and let cool slightly.

recipe and ingredients continue ☞

Garlicky Mayonnaise

1 large pasteurized egg (or ¼ cup / 60ml pasteurized liquid egg)

1 tablespoon fresh lemon juice (from about half a lemon)

1 tablespoon white vinegar

3 garlic cloves, peeled

Kosher salt

¾ cup / 175ml neutral oil, such as canola or vegetable

WHILE THE FRIES ARE ROASTING, MAKE THE GARLICKY MAYONNAISE: Combine the egg, lemon juice, vinegar, garlic, and ½ teaspoon of salt in a blender and blend on medium-low speed until the garlic is broken down and the mixture is completely smooth, about 30 seconds. With the blender running, slowly pour in the oil. At first the mixture will look lumpy and broken, but after 30 to 60 seconds the mayonnaise will come together. As soon as the mayonnaise is smooth, turn off the blender. Taste for seasoning and add more salt if needed.

Top the fries with freshly grated Parmesan cheese (if using) and serve with the mayonnaise.

NOTES: Feel free to use any hearty herb in place of the rosemary on the fries. Finely chopped thyme or sage would work well. And if herbs aren't your thing, you can omit them altogether.

To make a quicker garlicky mayonnaise, combine 1 cup / 240g of store-bought mayonnaise, 3 minced garlic cloves, 1 tablespoon of fresh lemon juice (from about half a lemon), and ¼ teaspoon of kosher salt in a small bowl and stir until well blended.

Bad Aim Chicken

Say you're hosting a dinner party in your extraplanar mansion, and you're serving a lot of chicken—pretty much *only* chicken, in fact. Some of your guests start complaining, wanting more variety in their meal. Then another guest starts flying around on her broomstick, shooting arrows, resulting in one skewered chicken on your wall and one puncture wound on your neck. What's a gracious, talented, seriously injured host to do? Hypothetically speaking, of course. Well, you could turn lemons into lemonade. No, for real, go find a lemon—also some pineapple and onion, and maybe some yogurt, stuff like that—and make these marinated chicken skewers. Oh, and bandage that neck wound. Yikes.

**PREP TIME: 4 hours
45 minutes
COOK TIME: 15 minutes**

---

1 cup / 128g fresh cilantro

1 cup / 128g parsley

2 jalapeňo chiles, stemmed and seeded

2 garlic cloves, peeled

Zest and juice of 1 lemon

3 tablespoons olive oil

½ cup / 120g plain, full-fat Greek yogurt

1 tablespoon ground cumin, toasted

1 tablespoon ground coriander seeds, toasted

4 to 6 boneless, skinless chicken thighs, cut into ½-inch cubes

1 pineapple, cut into ½-inch cubes

8 green onions, cut into 2-inch pieces

Kosher salt and freshly ground black pepper

In a blender, add the cilantro, parsley, jalapeño chiles, garlic, lemon zest and juice, olive oil, and yogurt and blend until a smooth mixture forms, about 1 minute. Pour out half of the yogurt mixture into a small serving bowl and refrigerate to use for dipping sauce later. Add the ground cumin and coriander seeds to the remaining mixture and blend until a smooth marinade forms.

Place the chicken in a sealable food-safe container and cover with the yogurt marinade, making sure all the cubes are generously coated. Place in the fridge to marinate for 4 to 24 hours.

Take out the chicken an hour before grilling and heat a grill or plancha on high.

While the grill is heating, assemble the kebabs on metal skewers, alternating chicken, pineapple cubes, and green onions. With the green onions, stack 3 or 4 pieces in a bundled section, so there is a sizable bite of green onion in between the chicken and pineapple. Season with salt and pepper.

recipe continues ☞

Cook on the grill or plancha until the chicken releases from the surface without tearing, 2 to 3 minutes.

Flip the skewers and cook until the chicken reaches a temperature of 165°F / 75°C and the juices run clear, 2 to 3 more minutes.

Remove the dipping sauce from the refrigerator 30 minutes before serving and allow to reach room temperature. Season with salt and pepper and serve with the chicken skewers.

Hidden Hospitality Fry Bread

One of our researchers, upon returning from an expedition through the Rifenmist Jungle, found an unexpected piece of parchment in her bag. A note at the top read, "From Niirdal-Poc: Elam says 'you're welcome.'" We have heard only rumors of Niirdal-Poc: an ancient city, deep in the jungle, hidden from travelers unless the city chooses to reveal itself to them. While some have questioned the parchment page's authenticity, its recipe for this very tasty fry bread is the real deal. And, should this truly be a missive from Niirdal-Poc itself, who are we to refuse such a rare gift? So, if you're out there, Elam: Thank you.

PREP TIME: 45 minutes
COOK TIME: 30 minutes

Plum and Coffee Chutney

4 firm medium plums, peeled, pitted, and medium diced

2 medium Jonagold or Honeycrisp apples, peeled, cored, and medium diced

⅓ cup / 80ml apple cider vinegar

¼ cup / 60ml water

3 tablespoons dark brown sugar

Zest and juice of 1 small lemon

1 tablespoon instant coffee

½ tablespoon ground cinnamon

1 star anise pod

1 cardamom pod

½ teaspoon vanilla bean powder

To make the plum and coffee chutney: In a medium heavy-bottomed pot, combine the plums, apples, apple cider vinegar, water, brown sugar, lemon zest and juice, instant coffee, cinnamon, anise, cardamom, and vanilla bean powder. Bring to a boil over high heat, then turn down the heat to low and simmer, stirring occasionally, until the chutney begins to break down slightly and thicken, 12 to 20 minutes. The chutney should be glossy, thick, and somewhat chunky. Let cool to room temperature and remove the cardamom and star anise pods.

To make the fry bread: In a large heavy-bottomed saucepan, heat the oil over high heat to 375°F/ 190°C. Once hot, lower the heat to medium-high. Flour a nonporous surface and line a plate with paper towels.

While the oil heats, in a medium bowl sift together 1 cup / 128g of the flour and the baking powder and salt. Once combined, add the milk and knead together until a smooth dough forms, 3 to 5 minutes. If the dough is too sticky, gradually add the remaining ½ cup / 64g of flour until the dough is pliable.

Fry Bread

3 cups / 710ml sunflower oil

1½ cups / 210g all-purpose flour, plus more for dusting

½ tablespoon baking powder

¼ teaspoon kosher salt

½ cup / 120ml milk

1 cup / 240ml crème fraîche or whipped cream (optional)

Place the dough on the floured surface and divide it into four pieces. Using a rolling pin, roll out 5-inch / 13cm rounds and carefully add them to the hot oil.

Fry on one side until golden, 1 to 2 minutes. Using a spider skimmer or a slotted spoon, flip over and fry on the other side until golden, for an additional 1 to 2 minutes.

Place the finished breads on the paper towels to absorb excess oil.

While the fry bread is hot, spoon a generous serving of plum and coffee chutney over the bread, add a dollop of crème fraîche or whipped cream (if using), and serve.

NOTE: If not consumed immediately, the chutney can be stored in a sterilized, airtight glass jar and refrigerated for up to 2 weeks.

De Rolos Revenge Pasta

For generations, the traditional dish of the de Rolos, rulers of the city of Whitestone, was a warming pasta puttanesca. Then the Briarwoods took over the city, slaughtered all but two of the de Rolos, and reigned for years of gloom and terror. After the survivors, Percy and his sister Cassandra, reclaimed Whitestone with Vox Machina's help, some old traditions were bound to evolve. Now a new dish has been added to the celebratory rotation. The topping is white, like Percy's hair, rather than the red of blood, and the pasta contains two entire heads of garlic. Partake in good health and stinky breath. Unless you're a vampire, in which case: go straight to hell, and say hi to the Briarwoods for us.

PREP TIME: 10 minutes
COOK TIME: 20 minutes

———

Kosher salt

1 pound / 450g dried spaghetti

½ cup / 120ml extra-virgin olive oil, plus more for serving

20 garlic cloves, thinly sliced (about ½ cup / 100g)

½ teaspoon crushed red pepper flakes

Freshly ground black pepper

⅓ cup / 15g finely chopped fresh parsley leaves (from about 1 small bunch)

1½ cups / 360g whole milk ricotta cheese

Bring a large pot of generously salted water to a boil over high heat. Add the spaghetti and cook according to the package instructions, 9 to 12 minutes. Drain in a colander.

Heat the olive oil in the now-empty pot over medium heat. Add the garlic and red pepper flakes and cook, stirring often, until the garlic is very fragrant and soft, 2½ to 3½ minutes. Remove the pot from the heat and add the cooked spaghetti, 1 teaspoon of salt, ½ teaspoon of black pepper, and the parsley. Toss the pasta to evenly coat it with the infused oil.

Transfer the pasta onto serving plates and top each portion with a generous dollop of ricotta cheese. Drizzle with olive oil and finish with additional black pepper.

Gem of Byroden Festival

If you're traveling between the Rifenmist Peninsula and the rest of Tal'Dorei, you'll likely pass through a sprawling settlement in which a surprising number of the residents go about their days fully armed. This is Byroden, former home of Vox Machina's Vex'ahlia and Vax'ildan. Byroden is known for three M's: militia, mining, and merriment. And if you happen to stop by during the annual Gem of Byroden pageant, you will experience a shining example of the third.

The main event is the pageant itself, in which anyone who wishes may compete to win the title of Gem of Byroden. Complementing the pageantry is a food competition, and the theme of the daytime competition is pies. There are so many pies presented that, if we could convince the bakers to part with their secrets, the recipes would fill this entire book. Instead, we have chosen three recipes that will give you a taste of the day.

First up, our Sweet Tea Custard Pie pays tribute to the only nonalcoholic drink available at the festival.* Then there's the Chicken Pocket Pie—if you're worried about getting full, just stash it away for later! Last, we could not pass up the opportunity to bring you Byroden's own Berry Surprise.** We, and the fine folks of Byroden, hope these treats will persuade you to make the journey for yourself. Bring your appetite and your sauciest evening wear, and the next Gem of Byroden could be you!

*You read that right. They will not serve you water. Enjoy the tea.

**Sample responsibly; the "surprise" is rum.

recipe continues ☞

Sweet Tea Custard Pie

PREP TIME: 20 minutes
COOK TIME: 2 hours

Pie Dough

1½ cups / 210g all-purpose flour, plus more for dusting

2 tablespoons granulated sugar

½ teaspoon kosher salt

½ cup (1 stick) / 110g cold unsalted butter, cut into ½-inch cubes

2 tablespoons ice water, plus more as needed

Sweet Tea Custard

1½ cups / 360ml heavy cream

1 cup / 240ml whole milk

1 tablespoon vanilla extract

½ teaspoon kosher salt

5 unflavored single-serving black tea bags (see Note)

4 large eggs

1 cup / 200g granulated sugar

TO MAKE THE PIE DOUGH: Lightly flour a work surface. In a large bowl, combine the flour, granulated sugar, and salt. Add the butter and use your fingertips or a pastry cutter to pinch the cubes into the flour until the butter is roughly the size of peas and no large chunks remain. Add the ice water and mix just until the dough starts to come together. The dough should hold together when squeezed. If the dough is too dry, add additional ice water, 1 teaspoon at a time, until it comes together.

Turn out the dough onto the floured surface and form it into a disk. Roll out into a 13-inch / 33cm circle about ¼ inch thick. Transfer the crust to a 9-inch / 23cm pie pan and press the dough into the bottom and sides. Trim the excess dough hanging around the edges, leaving a 1-inch / 2.5cm overhang all around the rim, then roll the edge under itself and crimp with your fingers to create a scalloped edge. Prick the bottom and sides of the crust several times with a fork. Place the crust in the freezer for 20 minutes.

Set a rack in the middle of the oven and preheat to 350°F / 175°C. Lay a sheet of parchment paper over the chilled crust and fill with pie weights or dry beans. Place the pie pan on a baking sheet and bake until the edges of the crust are just starting to brown, 20 to 25 minutes. Remove the pie weights and parchment paper and bake until the bottom no longer looks wet, 5 to 7 minutes more. Let the crust cool while you prepare the custard.

TO MAKE THE SWEET TEA CUSTARD: In a medium pot, combine the cream, milk, vanilla, and salt. Bring the mixture to a simmer over medium heat, 5 to 7 minutes. Decrease the heat to low and add the tea bags. Stir to completely submerge the tea bags and simmer for 15 minutes, stirring often, to

recipe and ingredients continue ☞

Whipped Cream Topping

2 cups / 475ml heavy cream

½ cup / 60g confectioners' sugar

1 teaspoon vanilla extract

Lemon zest, for garnish (optional)

allow the tea to infuse. Meanwhile, in a large heatproof bowl combine the eggs and granulated sugar and whisk until the mixture is thick and slightly lightened in color.

Remove the tea bags from the milk mixture and discard. While whisking the egg mixture, use a dry measuring cup or ladle to slowly add the hot milk mixture into the egg mixture. Pour the custard into the parbaked crust. Bake the pie until the custard is completely set around the edges but slightly wobbly in the center, 35 to 40 minutes. If the crust starts to brown before the custard is cooked, crimp a large piece of foil around the edges to prevent further browning.

Let the pie cool at room temperature for 1 hour, then refrigerate for at least 4 hours and preferably overnight.

WHEN READY TO SERVE, MAKE THE WHIPPED CREAM TOPPING: In the bowl of a stand mixer fitted with a whisk attachment, combine the heavy cream, confectioners' sugar, and vanilla extract. (Alternatively, use a large mixing bowl and electric handheld mixer.) Beat on medium-high speed for 2 to 3 minutes, until soft peaks form. Transfer the whipped cream to the top of the pie and spread out in an even layer. Garnish with lemon zest, if using.

NOTE: Any unflavored black tea—English Breakfast, Irish Breakfast, or Ceylon—works well in this recipe. If using loose leaf tea, use 5 teaspoons of leaves in place of the 5 tea bags and strain the milk mixture through a fine-mesh strainer before adding to the eggs.

Chicken Pocket Pies

PREP TIME: 1 hour
COOK TIME: 1 hour

Pie Dough

3 cups / 420g all-purpose flour, plus more for dusting

1 teaspoon kosher salt

1 cup (2 sticks) / 220g cold unsalted butter, cut into ½-inch cubes

¼ cup / 60ml ice water, plus more as needed

1 large egg

Filling

1 pound / 450g boneless, skinless chicken breasts (about 2 large breasts), cut into ½-inch cubes

Kosher salt and freshly ground black pepper

2 tablespoons olive oil

4 tablespoons / 55g unsalted butter

1½ cups / 210g diced yellow onion (from about 1 large onion)

⅔ cup / 75g diced celery (from about 2 stalks)

⅔ cup / 90g peeled and diced carrot (from about 1 large carrot)

TO MAKE THE PIE DOUGH: Lightly flour a work surface. In a large bowl, combine the flour and salt. Add the butter and use your fingertips or a pastry cutter to pinch the cubes into the flour until the butter is roughly the size of peas and no large chunks remain. Add the ice water and mix just until the dough starts to come together. The dough should hold together when squeezed. If the dough is too dry, add additional ice water, 1 teaspoon at a time, until it comes together.

Turn out the dough onto the floured surface and shape it into a flat disk. Wrap it in plastic wrap and chill in the refrigerator for at least 1 hour and up to 3 days.

TO MAKE THE FILLING: In a medium bowl, combine the chicken and 1 teaspoon each of salt and pepper and toss to evenly coat. Heat the olive oil in a large pot or Dutch oven over medium heat until shimmering. Add the chicken and cook, stirring occasionally, until lightly browned and cooked through, 6 to 9 minutes. Transfer the chicken to a plate and set aside.

Melt the butter in the pot and add the onion, celery, and carrot. Cook, stirring often, until the onion is translucent, 5 to 7 minutes. Add the garlic and thyme and continue cooking until fragrant, 1 to 2 minutes more. Sprinkle on the flour, stir to evenly coat the vegetables, and cook just until no pockets of dry flour remain, about 1 minute. Slowly add the milk while stirring and bring the mixture up to a simmer. Remove the pot from the heat and stir in the chicken and peas. Taste for seasoning and add additional salt and pepper if needed. Transfer the filling to a baking pan or large plate and spread out in an even layer. Refrigerate for 1 hour to firm up.

3 garlic cloves, minced

2 teaspoons chopped fresh thyme leaves (from about 10 sprigs)

¼ cup / 35g all-purpose flour

2 cups / 475ml whole milk

½ cup / 65g frozen peas

While the filling is cooling, line a baking sheet with parchment paper or a nonstick baking mat. Lightly flour a work surface. Crack the egg into a small bowl and whisk until no streaks of yolk remain.

Unwrap the dough, set it on the floured surface, and roll it out into a ⅛-inch-thick sheet. Using a 5-inch / 13cm round cutter, cut out ten circles of dough. Place a heaping ¼ cup / 70g of the filling in the center of each round, leaving a ½-inch border around the edge. Brush the outside edge of the dough with egg and fold the dough over the filling to create a half moon shape. Pinch the edges to seal and crimp with a fork or your fingers to create a scalloped edge. Transfer the pocket pies onto the prepared baking sheet, spacing them 1 inch / 2.5cm apart, and slash the top of each pie three times with a knife. Transfer the baking sheet to the freezer and freeze for 30 minutes.

Set a rack in the middle of the oven and preheat to 375°F / 190°C. Brush the pies with the remaining egg wash and bake until light golden brown, 38 to 42 minutes. Remove from the oven and let cool on the baking sheet.

Scanlan's Hand Pies

Have you heard tell of Scanlan the grand,
With the most famous voice in the land?
As a gnome, he's quite small,
But his spells? Not at all!
One can summon a huge purple hand!

Often, we heard the gnome give a sigh,
"There aren't enough Me Foods. But why?
Why can't the food I eat
Be inspired by my feats?"
So we made him this purple hand pie.

—Submitted by the kitchen staff of the Laughing Lamia Inn in Emon,
at the repeated and insistent behest of Master Shorthalt by popular demand

PREP TIME: 55 minutes
COOK TIME: 1 hour

———

Pie Dough

3 cups / 420g all-purpose flour, plus more for dusting

¼ cup / 50g granulated sugar

1 teaspoon kosher salt

1 cup (2 sticks) / 220g cold unsalted butter, cut into ½-inch cubes

¼ cup / 60ml ice water, plus more as needed

1 large egg

To make the pie dough: Lightly flour a work surface. In a large bowl, combine the flour, granulated sugar, and salt. Add the butter and use your fingertips or a pastry cutter to pinch the cubes into the flour until the butter is roughly the size of peas and no large chunks remain. Add the ice water and mix just until the dough starts to come together. The dough should hold together when squeezed. If the dough is too dry, add additional ice water, 1 teaspoon at a time, until it comes together.

Turn out the dough onto the floured surface. Cut the dough in half and form each half into a disk. Wrap both halves in plastic wrap and chill for at least 1 hour and up to 3 days.

Blackberry Filling

2 teaspoons cornstarch

1 tablespoon cold water

12 ounces / 340g blackberries (about 3 cups)

¾ cup / 150g granulated sugar

3 tablespoons lemon juice (from about 1 large lemon)

1 tablespoon lemon zest (from about 1 large lemon)

2 teaspoons vanilla extract

¼ teaspoon kosher salt

Blackberry Glaze

3 ounces / 85g blackberries (about ¾ cup)

2 tablespoons water, plus more as needed

2 cups / 240g confectioners' sugar, plus more as needed

Purple sprinkles, for garnish (optional)

To make the blackberry filling: In a small bowl, combine the cornstarch and cold water and stir until dissolved. Set aside.

In a large saucepan, combine the blackberries, granulated sugar, lemon juice and zest, vanilla, and salt. Cook over medium heat, stirring often and occasionally smashing the berries, until the berries are completely broken down and the mixture thickens into a syrup-like consistency, 15 to 18 minutes. Stir in the cornstarch mixture and continue cooking until the mixture thickens into a jam-like consistency that coats the back of the spoon, 1 to 2 minutes. Remove from the heat and let cool at room temperature for at least 20 minutes.

Line a baking sheet with parchment paper or a nonstick baking mat. Crack the egg into a small bowl and whisk until no streaks of yolk remain.

Unwrap one disk of dough and set it on the floured surface. Dust the top of the dough with flour and roll out into a 9 by 12-inch / 23 by 30cm rectangle about ¼ inch thick. Trim the edges so they are straight and cut the rectangle into a 3 by 3 grid to make nine rectangles that are roughly 3 by 4 inches / 7.5 by 10cm. Transfer the rectangles onto the prepared baking sheet, spacing them at least 1 inch / 2.5cm apart. Spread 2 tablespoons of the filling in the center of each rectangle, leaving a ½-inch border around the edge. Repeat the rolling and cutting process with the second disk of dough to make 9 more rectangles.

Brush the outside borders of the filled rectangles with the egg wash (reserve the remaining egg wash) and place the unfilled rectangles on top. Crimp the edges together with a fork and prick the tops a few times. Transfer the pan to the freezer and freeze for 30 minutes.

recipe continues ☞

Position a rack in the middle of the oven and preheat to 375°F / 190°C. Brush the pies with the remaining egg wash. Bake, rotating the pan halfway through baking, until light golden brown, 28 to 32 minutes. Remove from the oven and let cool completely on the baking sheet.

WHILE THE HAND PIES ARE COOLING, MAKE THE BLACKBERRY GLAZE: Place the blackberries and water in a blender and blend until smooth. Strain the mixture through a fine-mesh strainer into a medium bowl and discard the pulp and seeds. Add the confectioners' sugar and whisk until completely dissolved. The glaze should be thick but pourable. If too thin, whisk in an additional tablespoon of confectioners' sugar. If too thick, whisk in an additional teaspoon of water.

Glaze the top of each hand pie with the glaze and sprinkle the tops with the sprinkles, if using. Let set for at least 30 minutes before serving.

2

ISSYLRA

Issylra

Let's leave Tal'Dorei now, crossing the Ozmit Sea north and west, heading for Issylra, the birthplace of civilization. Before we can understand this storied land and its cuisine, we need to briefly review the long, awe-inspiring, often troubled relationship between Exandria, the gods, and magic. Of course, we at Exquisite Exandria are not authorities on the deep mysteries of the universe, so we'll begin with some sweeping generalities.

In the time of the Founding, the gods shaped the many peoples of Exandria, gifting them morsels of their divine power to help them survive. Magic was born. With the aid of magic, the mortal races developed tools to not just survive but thrive. Civilizations were founded, and the people of those civilizations remembered to thank the gods for their gifts. Organized religion was born.

The Founding, however, was not the beginning of Exandria's history. The gods found Exandria, already extant, with a race of elemental titans called the Primordials already living there. Angered with the gods, their people, and their meddling with the land, the Primordials rose up and attacked. The people called to their gods for help.

Some of the gods said no. They sided with the Primordials against their divine brethren, becoming what we now refer to as the Betrayer Gods. A terrible conflict followed, ending with the gods thereafter known as the Prime Deities locking the Betrayer Gods away in other planes of existence. Afterward, as civilization once again thrived, the people of Exandria knew for sure: These were gods that loved them. These were gods worthy of their loyalty.

But time passed, and people forgot. Magic flourished beyond all previous bounds, unlocking ever more secrets. Huge cities like Aeor and Avalir rose from the ground and flew. Arduous tasks could be accomplished in an eyeblink. What does being a god mean, when anyone who studies the arcane hard enough can stop time or create life? As civilization's thriving soured into indulgence, mortals decided they wanted to find out. Some attempted to become gods. One, the Matron of Ravens, even succeeded. In the misguided experimentation that followed, the Betrayer Gods were freed. God fought god once again, with disastrous results. During the Calamity that followed, at least two-thirds of the population of Exandria was killed, lands were left barren, and most traces of civilization were destroyed.

Except for Vasselheim. The rest of Issylra became, and largely remains, untamed wilderness, but Vasselheim survived. After banishing the Betrayer

Gods again, the Prime Deities chose to lock themselves beyond the Divine Gate, removing their ability to act directly upon Exandria. Vasselheim, the Dawn City, was where they made this announcement. Vasselheim was the last city standing after the gods warred, Vasselheim was where the gods departed this plane of existence, and Vasselheim, the people swore, was where the gods would be forever remembered.

After the departure of the gods, an event known as the Divergence, many things started anew. The calendar, to name one example, began counting years PD, "Post Divergence." But Vasselheim endured, Vasselheim remembered, and that continues to this day.

Vasselheim refuses to make the mistakes of its ancestors. Arcane magic—the kind not directly inspired by the divine, the kind that brought about the Calamity—is banned within the city. Each of the major sections of the city is dedicated to a Prime Deity: the Abundant Terrace to the Wildmother, goddess of nature; the Quadroads to the Lawbearer, goddess of civilization; the Braving Grounds to the Stormlord, god of glory and strength; the Silver Talon's Reach to the Platinum Dragon, god of justice and protection; and the Duskmeadow District to the Matron of Ravens, goddess of death. Other Prime Deities are also worshipped in temples across the city, such as the Dawnfather, god of the sun, summer, and time; the Changebringer, goddess of freedom and adventure; and the Everlight, goddess of compassion and redemption.

But now it's time to focus on the food. Issylra has always been a cold place of isolated settlements, so the cuisine has developed from that mentality. Even in times of plenty, food in such a place never stops being precious. Heavy emphasis is placed on hunting, marking the seasons, and avoiding waste, all to ensure that food stores are sufficient and life is sustained. But the people of Issylra also use meals as a form of worship. There are, of course, the celebratory feasts throughout the year to honor one or more of the Prime Deities. The food served at these religious meals is usually elaborate, requiring hours of preparation and meticulous attention. Especially in Vasselheim, though, most everyday dinners are also sit-down affairs, not necessarily somber, but certainly ritualized and formal. With each bite, whether consciously or subconsciously, the people of Vasselheim renew their vow. *We remember and thank the gods who saved us. We honor their magic and practice no other. We remember the hubris that nearly destroyed us. We will never forget again.*

In the following pages, we have collected a range of these commemorative dishes. For those times when you're in the mood to celebrate good company or a good harvest or if you just want to try some unusual cookies, home cooks and professional chefs across Issylra have opened their recipe books to help. All they ask is that you do as they do when they sit down to eat: Remember your blessings, and learn from your mistakes.

Highsummer Honey Polenta

Highsummer, the Dawnfather's holy day, is marked across Exandria with glorious feasts. In Vasselheim, festivities kick off on the Abundant Terrace—at dawn, of course—with freshly harvested corn and honey, made into this gorgeous polenta. The sun may be low in the sky, but its coming heat is celebrated by adding chiles to the honey. The adults linger over their bowls, debating whether to have seconds (or thirds) or pace themselves for the other treats to come, while the children compete to see how much spicy honey they can eat without breaking a sweat. Impending stomachaches aside, it is a lovely way to start an excellent day.

PREP TIME: 15 minutes
COOK TIME: 1 hour 15 minutes

___

4 ears fresh yellow corn, shucked

4 cups / 950ml water

One 14-ounce / 403ml can unsweetened coconut milk

Kosher salt and freshly ground black pepper

4 tablespoons / 55g unsalted butter

1 cup / 175g coarsely ground yellow polenta

1 large shallot, finely chopped

3 garlic cloves, minced

Spicy Citrus Honey (recipe follows), for drizzling

2 green onions, thinly sliced

Cut the kernels away from the corn cobs (about 4 cups / 600g) and set the kernels aside. Use a spoon or the back of a butter knife to scrape the "corn milk" off of the cobs and into a large saucepan. Break the scraped cobs in half and place in the saucepan along with the water. Bring to a boil over medium-high heat, then lower to a simmer and cook for 30 minutes. Remove the cobs and discard. Measure out the corn stock; you should have 2½ cups / 590ml. If you have less, add water to get to that amount; if you have more, ladle out the extra stock and reserve to thin out the polenta later (if needed).

Return the corn stock to the saucepan and stir in the coconut milk, 2 teaspoons salt, and several large grinds of black pepper. Bring to a simmer over medium heat, whisking occasionally so the coconut milk doesn't scorch. Slowly whisk in the polenta, then lower the heat slightly to maintain a gentle simmer. Cook, whisking frequently, until the polenta is tender and thick, about 20 minutes. If the polenta gets too thick before it is tender, whisk in a little bit of hot water (or extra corn stock if you have it). Whisk in 2 tablespoons of the butter, then remove from the heat. Cover the saucepan with a lid to keep the polenta warm and set aside.

In a large skillet set over just below medium-high heat, melt the remaining 2 tablespoons of butter. Add the shallot and cook, stirring occasionally, until softened, about 5 minutes. Add the garlic and cook, stirring constantly, until softened, about 2 minutes. Stir in the reserved corn kernels, season with salt and pepper, and increase the heat to medium-high. Cook, stirring frequently, until the corn is crisp-tender, 5 to 7 minutes.

Stir half of the sautéed corn into the hot polenta and season with additional salt and pepper. If needed, adjust the consistency of the polenta with additional hot water (or corn stock if you have it). It should be thick but pourable. Divide the polenta among four to six bowls, then top with the remaining sautéed corn, drizzle with some Spicy Citrus Honey, and garnish with the scallions. Serve immediately.

SPICY CITRUS HONEY

MAKES ABOUT 1 CUP / 240ML

PREP TIME: 5 minutes
COOK TIME: 20 minutes

---

1 to 3 (depending on your spice preference) Fresno chiles, thinly sliced

3 long strips of orange rind (4 to 5 inches / 10 to 13cm long)

¾ cup / 175ml clover honey

In a small saucepan over low heat, combine the chiles, orange rind, and honey and slowly bring almost to a simmer, swirling the saucepan occasionally. This should take close to 20 minutes (if not longer, depending on your stovetop). Once it comes to almost a simmer, immediately remove from the heat and cool the infused honey completely in the saucepan at room temperature. Transfer to a small jar with a tight-fitting lid and store in the refrigerator for up to 3 months.

Shorecomb Smørrebrød

Shorecomb is a port city, hundreds of miles southwest of Vasselheim, and a frequent stop for trade ships making their way along the Issylran coast. Its residents, therefore, were unprepared for the heroes of Vox Machina to magically emerge from a tree on the outskirts of town instead of arriving by boat. But powerful guests appearing out of nowhere to hunt down a freshly ascended god with little notice is no reason to be a bad host!

Smørrebrød is this coastal town's favorite gesture of hospitality. This open-faced sandwich showcases both the fresh and dried seafood of the region, and it can be adapted to include everything from a prized batch of fresh cheese to leftover potatoes, depending on the season, one's feelings about one's guests, and the suddenness with which they appear out of thin air.

recipe continues ☞

Cod and Potato Smørrebrød

PREP TIME: 2 hours
COOK TIME: 1 hour
30 minutes

Garlic Compound Butter

1 medium garlic head

¾ cup (1½ sticks) / 165g salted butter, at room temperature

1 tablespoon dried parsley flakes

Cod and Potato Purée

6 ounces / 170g dried cod

3 cups / 710ml water

½ cup / 120ml milk

3 medium or 1½ large russet potatoes, peeled and medium diced

Juice of 1 medium lemon

¼ cup / 60ml heavy cream

2 egg yolks

Kosher salt and freshly ground black pepper

NOTE: The Cod and Potato Purée must be started several days in advance.

To make the garlic compound butter: Preheat the oven to 400°F / 200°C. Leaving the garlic head intact, slice off the top and discard. Wrap the garlic in aluminum foil and roast in the oven for 20 minutes, until the garlic is soft.

Squeeze out the garlic cloves into a medium bowl and add the butter and parsley flakes. Gently fold the ingredients into one another until well incorporated, about 1 minute.

Store the butter in a small sealable container. It will keep, refrigerated, for up to 2 weeks.

To make the cod and potato purée: Two to 3 days before serving, submerge the dried cod in cold water in a medium glass or plastic bowl. Cover with a tea towel and leave on the counter. After 24 hours, change the water. Continue to change the water every day, until the cod is no longer salty.

When the cod is ready, in a medium pot, combine it with the 3 cups of water and ¼ cup / 60ml of the milk. Bring to a boil and quickly reduce to a simmer. Cook the cod until the flesh is rehydrated and flaky, 15 to 20 minutes.

Once cooked, drain the cod and flake it with a fork. Discard the skin and any residual bones. Set aside.

In a separate pot, cover the potatoes with cold water and bring to a boil. Do not salt. Cook until the potatoes are fork-tender, about 15 minutes. Once cooked, thoroughly drain, transfer to a medium mixing bowl, and mash using a fork or ricer until the potatoes are smooth and free of lumps.

recipe and ingredients continue ↦

Fried Capers

3 tablespoons olive oil

40 to 50 capers in brine, dried

For Assembly

1 loaf Nordic-style dark rye bread, cut into eight to ten ½-inch-thick slices

15 to 20 medium to large purple potato chips

Zest of 1 medium lemon

8 to 10 pea shoots

Kosher salt and freshly ground black pepper

1 lemon, cut into 6 to 8 wedges

Fold the flaked cod into the mashed potatoes until almost well combined.

Mix in the lemon juice, the remaining ¼ cup / 60ml of milk, the cream, and egg yolks until a thick, creamy purée forms. Season with salt and pepper.

Preheat the oven to 400°F / 200°C and line a baking sheet with parchment paper. Scoop the purée into a piping bag with a star nozzle.

On the prepared baking sheet, pipe small crowns of purée about 1 inch / 2.5cm in diameter, 1 inch / 2.5cm apart. Bake until the crowns turn a light golden brown, 5 to 10 minutes.

TO MAKE THE FRIED CAPERS: While the potato crowns are baking, line a plate with paper towels. Heat a medium saucepan over high heat. Lower the heat to medium and add the olive oil and capers. Fry the capers until crispy, about 2 minutes. Transfer the capers to the paper towel–lined plate to drain.

TO ASSEMBLE THE SMØRREBRØD: Slightly toast the rye bread. Generously spread the compound butter on one side, top with 4 to 6 potato crowns, and gently lay potato chips in between the crowns. On each slice, sprinkle 4 or 5 capers and some lemon zest, and top with pea shoots. Season with salt and pepper and serve with a wedge of lemon.

NOTE: If you want an even moister smørrebrød, drizzle a small amount of olive oil over the crowns before adding the potato chips.

Pickled Shrimp Smørrebrød

PREP TIME: 2 hours
COOK TIME: 20 minutes
———

2 cups / 475ml water

16 to 20 extra jumbo shrimp, uncooked, cleaned, and peeled

½ tablespoon celery seeds

½ tablespoon mustard seeds

2 garlic cloves, peeled

1 tablespoon pink peppercorns

⅓ cup / 80ml dill aquavit

1 large lemon, cut into ¼-inch-thick wedges

½ cup / 120ml canola oil

½ cup / 120ml apple cider vinegar

2 tablespoons granulated sugar

½ teaspoon kosher salt

Herbed Whipped Feta

One 8-ounce / 225g block of feta, at room temperature

⅓ cup / 80g cream cheese

⅓ cup / 80ml olive oil

1 bunch chives, finely chopped

Kosher salt and freshly ground black pepper

Prepare an ice bath. In a medium pot over medium heat, heat the water to 160°F / 71°C. Once hot, submerge the shrimp in the hot water until slightly pink but still gray and undercooked, about 30 seconds. Immediately plunge the shrimp into the ice bath to stop further cooking.

Drain the shrimp and transfer to a large sterilized, sealable jar with the celery seeds, mustard seeds, garlic, peppercorns, dill aquavit, lemon wedges, canola oil, apple cider vinegar, sugar, and salt. Seal the jar and give it a few shakes to distribute the ingredients. Refrigerate for at least 12 hours and up to 24 hours.

When done, the shrimp should be completely pink, tangy, and have a firm bite, but not be rubbery.

TO MAKE THE HERBED WHIPPED FETA: An hour before serving, whip the feta with a stand or electric handheld mixer on medium-high speed. While whipping, add the cream cheese, olive oil, and chives, one at a time, so each gets well incorporated. Season with salt and pepper.

Spoon the whipped feta into a piping bag with a nozzle and set aside.

recipe and ingredients continue ☞

Roasted Cherry Tomatoes

18 to 20 cherry tomatoes, halved lengthwise

3 tablespoons olive oil

Kosher salt and freshly ground black pepper

For Assembly

1 loaf Nordic-style dark rye bread, cut into eight to ten ½-inch-thick slices

Garlic Compound Butter (page 83)

Torn fresh basil

Kosher salt and freshly ground black pepper

4 to 6 lemon wedges

To make the roasted cherry tomatoes: Preheat the oven to 400°F / 200°C and line a baking sheet with parchment paper. Place the tomatoes on the baking sheet, drizzle with the olive oil, and gently toss so the tomatoes are evenly coated. Season with salt and pepper.

Roast the tomatoes until they are slightly charred and burst, 15 to 20 minutes.

To assemble the smørrebrød: Lightly toast the rye bread and generously spread the compound butter on one side. Pipe 3 or 4 feta nests asymmetrically on each toast. Gently lay 2 shrimp in between the nests and top with 3 or 4 cherry tomatoes. Top with torn basil, season with salt and pepper, and serve with lemon wedges.

Scaldseat Salmon

Another celebratory treat in Shorecomb is salmon, usually trolled from the Ozmit Sea in the hot, still days of Sydenstar, before the fish begin their yearly migration to the nearby rivers. During the day, the fisherfolk can sometimes navigate by a column of smoke rising from the water five miles off the coast. This smoke marks the location of the underwater volcano Scaldseat. This popular dinnertime presentation honors both the volcano and the end-of-summer bounty: Scaldseat Salmon, broiled to a char with freshly harvested lemons and honey.

PREP TIME: 15 minutes
COOK TIME: 30 minutes
——

¼ cup / 60ml olive oil

2 tablespoons honey

1 tablespoon finely chopped fresh dill, plus more for garnish

1 tablespoon fresh lemon juice (from about half a lemon)

1 teaspoon Dijon mustard

2 garlic cloves, minced

1 teaspoon kosher salt

½ teaspoon freshly ground black pepper

2 medium lemons, thinly sliced and seeded

One 3-pound / 1.4kg skin-on side of salmon

Position a rack in the upper third of the oven (about 6 inches / 15cm from the broiler) and preheat to 425°F / 220°C. Line a baking sheet with aluminum foil.

In a medium bowl, combine 2 tablespoons of the olive oil with the honey, dill, lemon juice, mustard, garlic, salt, and pepper. Whisk until the mustard is completely dissolved and the mixture is emulsified. In a separate medium bowl, toss the lemon slices with the remaining 2 tablespoons of olive oil to coat them.

Place the salmon on a large plate or cutting board. Pour the olive oil mixture over the salmon and rub the salmon so it's evenly coated on both sides. Arrange a thin layer of about 8 of the lemon slices in the center of the baking sheet. Place the salmon skin side down in the center of the baking sheet on top of the lemon slices and scatter the remaining lemon slices on top.

Bake just until the outside of the salmon has started to turn light pink, 8 to 10 minutes. Turn the oven off and set the broiler to high. Broil, rotating the pan halfway through, until the salmon is dark golden brown and the lemons have started to char, 10 to 12 minutes. Make sure to keep an eye on the salmon, as it browns very quickly. Remove the salmon from the oven, garnish with additional dill, and serve immediately.

Slayer's Take Stew

In the center of Vasselheim, the folk of the Quadroads come together on the autumnal equinox to celebrate the Lawbearer, the goddess of civilization and order. Giving gifts to the community is traditional on Civilization's Dawn, and the Slayer's Take guild outdo themselves year after year by presenting gorgeous cuts of meat from their hunts. A huge cooking pot is hoisted over one of the celebratory bonfires, and soon the smell of tasty meats and vegetables fills the air. Two hours (and some dedicated stirring) later, the resulting stew is ladled into bowls and handed around to all comers. We have taken the spirit of this stew and delivered it to you without the need for a waist-high cooking pot or a dangerous hunting trip into the Vesper Timberland.

PREP TIME: 25 minutes
COOK TIME: 2 hours

———

0.7 ounce / 20g (about 1 cup) dried mushrooms, such as porcini or shiitake

2 cups / 475ml boiling water

1 pound / 450g thick-cut bacon, diced

14 ounces / 400g kielbasa or other smoked sausage, cut into ¼-inch-thick rounds

1 pound / 450g cremini or white button mushrooms, trimmed and cut into quarters or eighths depending on size

3 cups / 420g diced yellow onions (from about 2 large onions)

2 large carrots, peeled and sliced into ¼-inch-thick rounds (about 1¾ cups / 210g)

Place the dried mushrooms in a medium heatproof bowl and pour the boiling water over them. Let sit at room temperature for at least 30 minutes.

While the mushrooms are rehydrating, add the bacon to a large heavy-bottomed pot or Dutch oven over medium heat. Cook, stirring often, until the bacon is crispy and has rendered all of its fat, 10 to 12 minutes. Remove the bacon from the pot using a slotted spoon and transfer to a medium bowl. Add the sliced kielbasa to the pot and cook, stirring often, until lightly browned, 4 to 7 minutes. Transfer the kielbasa into the bowl with the bacon using a slotted spoon. Remove ¼ cup / 60ml of the rendered fat and set aside.

Add the cremini mushrooms to the pot and cook, stirring often, until they release all of their liquid and begin to brown, 12 to 14 minutes. If at any point they get too brown and start sticking to the bottom of the pot, add ¼ cup / 60ml water and scrape loose the sticking bits.

recipe and ingredients continue ↦

5 garlic cloves, minced

¼ cup / 65g tomato paste

1 cup / 240ml dry red wine, such as Pinot Noir or Merlot

2 teaspoons paprika, preferably smoked

Kosher salt

1 teaspoon freshly ground black pepper

1 teaspoon caraway seeds

2 cups / 100g finely shredded green cabbage (from about one-third of a small head of cabbage)

1 pound / 450g sauerkraut, drained and rinsed (about 2 cups)

One 14.5-ounce / 411g can diced tomatoes

4 cups / 950ml low-sodium beef stock

2 dried bay leaves

Fresh dill, for garnish

Crusty bread, cooked egg noodles, or mashed potatoes, for serving

Add the onions and carrots and cook, stirring often, until the onions are soft and translucent, 6 to 9 minutes. If the onions look dry, add the reserved rendered fat. Add the garlic and tomato paste and cook until the tomato paste darkens slightly and starts sticking to the bottom of the pot, 4 to 7 minutes. Add the wine and cook, stirring constantly while scraping the bottom of the pot to dissolve any brown bits, until the wine reduces and the mixture is mostly dry, 3 to 5 minutes. Add the cooked sausage and bacon to the pot along with the paprika, 1½ teaspoons salt, the pepper, caraway, cabbage, sauerkraut, diced tomatoes with their juices, beef stock, and bay leaves.

Remove the dried mushrooms from the water (reserving the water) and roughly chop them. Add both the dried mushrooms and the soaking liquid to the pot. Bring the mixture to a simmer and cook uncovered, stirring occasionally, until the cabbage is wilted and the carrots are tender, 50 to 60 minutes.

Remove the bay leaves and taste the soup for seasoning. Garnish with fresh dill and serve with crusty bread, cooked egg noodles, or mashed potatoes.

Gunpowder Green Tea Shortbread Cookies

While we were gathering recipes for this book, we met a strange man in the Braving Grounds who said that, years back, he had eaten cookies made of gunpowder and found them delicious. "Gunpowder," our researcher replied. "Like tea, right? The green tea called gunpowder? That's what was in the cookies?" All they got in return was an eyebrow waggle and a ". . . sure." After some trial and much error,* we have concluded that he *had* to mean tea. So here are some tasty shortbread cookies flavored with gunpowder. Tea. Gunpowder tea.

Do not eat actual gunpowder. Learn from our mistakes.

PREP TIME: 15 minutes
COOK TIME: 25 minutes

———

2 tablespoons loose leaf gunpowder green tea (see Note)

2½ cups / 300g sifted all-purpose flour

½ teaspoon kosher salt

1 cup (2 sticks) / 220g unsalted butter, softened

1⅓ cups / 135g sifted confectioners' sugar

1 tablespoon vanilla extract

1 large egg

3 tablespoons coarse sugar, such as turbinado, Demerara, or sanding

Place the tea in a spice grinder or high-power blender and grind into a very fine powder, 40 to 60 seconds. (Alternatively, grind the tea in a blender or food processor and pass through a fine-mesh strainer to remove any large pieces.) Transfer the ground tea to a medium mixing bowl and add the flour and salt. Whisk to evenly distribute the tea powder throughout the flour.

In the bowl of a stand mixer fitted with the paddle attachment, combine the butter, confectioners' sugar, and vanilla. (Alternatively, use a large mixing bowl and an electric handheld mixer.) Beat on medium speed until smooth and fluffy, scraping the sides of the bowl halfway through, 2 to 3 minutes. Turn the mixer off and add the flour mixture. Mix on low speed just until a crumbly dough forms, 1 to 2 minutes.

Transfer the dough to a large sheet of plastic wrap. Form the dough into a 1½-inch / 4cm diameter log and tightly wrap it in the plastic, twisting the ends to help form a cylinder shape. Chill in the freezer for 1 hour, rotating every 15 minutes to help the dough keep its shape.

While the dough is chilling, crack the egg into a small mixing bowl and stir with a fork until no streaks of yolk remain. Line a baking sheet with parchment paper or a nonstick baking

recipe continues 🖝

mat and arrange a rack in the middle of the oven. Preheat to 350°F / 175°C.

Unwrap the chilled dough and brush the outside with the egg. Sprinkle the coarse sugar onto the sides of the log, gently pressing it in to help it stick. Use a sharp knife to slice the log into ½-inch-thick slices (about sixteen slices). Arrange the slices on the prepared baking sheet, spacing them about 1 inch / 2.5cm apart. (The cookies don't spread much.)

Bake the cookies until fragrant and the tops are completely matte, 18 to 23 minutes. Remove from the oven and let cool completely on the baking sheet.

NOTE: Gunpowder tea is a variety of tea (usually green tea) in which the leaves are tightly rolled into tiny pellets. The tea can be found in specialty coffee and tea stores or easily ordered online. If unavailable, any loose leaf green tea variety can be used instead.

3
MARQUET

MARQUET

Now we travel south, away from the cold wilderness of Issylra to a continent of very different extremes: Marquet.

Pre-Divergence, Marquet was lush from coast to coast, a mix of dense jungles and arable plains. The Calamity changed the nature of much of the land here, as it did elsewhere. Weird magics twisted the jungles into dangerous fey-touched wilderness, shattered the plains into jagged mountain ranges, and obliterated the settlements. One elven city in particular, Cael Morrow in the northeast, drew the wrath of the Betrayer God known as the Ruiner. He drove his spear clean through the city and the ground below, detonating a third of the continent in one gigantic strike. The cities and jungles that were in the way exploded into rubble and dust, which settled to become the sands of the Rumedam Desert.

Given this disastrous change— destruction all around, the loss of most staple food sources, and altered landscapes that were now actively trying to kill the inhabitants in many new ways—the people of Marquet responded with variations on a theme: exploration. Some left the continent entirely and struck out across the seas, founding the settlements that would become the Menagerie Coast in Wildemount, and financing the growth of Emon in Tal'Dorei. But many Marquesians set out to explore their old home anew.

Crossing the newly formed desert, hopeful traders discovered an oasis at the former site of Cael Morrow. They sunk wells and established caravan routes. Travelers began to arrive and to stay. What began as a simple trade post soon grew into a thriving community— and just as soon after, it began to descend into thievery and abuse. Then a mysterious, seemingly immortal figure named J'mon Sa Ord appeared and brought the city into order. Ank'Harel, meaning "Jewel of Hope" in Marquesian, was officially founded under their leadership. J'mon Sa Ord has ruled there ever since, providing the stability and protection that has allowed Ank'Harel to flower into the cultural center of the continent.

Striking into the Oderan Wilds in the northwest, explorers found five huge rock spires rising from the dense canopy. Some theorize that the spires were once a single mountain, rent during the Calamity. Other fanciful souls tell tales of a stone titan buried beneath the earth, with only the fingers of one hand left sticking aboveground to mark their passing. Whatever the case, the spires offered stable land above the dangerous jungle floor, and rock rich with metal, ore, and gems. Builders and miners went up and into the spires, and the city of Jrusar was born.

The nature of these two cities, both trading hubs—one a desert oasis and the other an oasis of rock amid the wild jungle—made them natural melting pots. Both cities opened skyports, allowing safer travel along the trade routes, and both drew settlers from across Marquet and eventually across Exandria. These settlers naturally brought their cultures with them: their worship, their dress, their language, and their food.

Some stayed in the cities. Others struck out, continuing to explore and reclaim the continent. Deeper in the Oderan Wilds, settlements like Heartmoor Hamlet used the jungle to their advantage in growing new crops, while the most adventurous settlers began tasting the fruits of the odd, fey-touched trees. Across the Rumedam to the north, at the base of the Aggrad Mountains, is the Bay of Gifts. The mild weather and sandy beaches make that stretch of coast perfect for a port and also a vacation, and the city of Shammel was born to serve both needs. Across Marquet, settlements took hold once again, in friendly and unfriendly land

alike, driven by the spirit of exploration and experimentation.

You don't have to look far to find that spirit infusing the cuisine of this amazing continent. Forests full of bizarre fruit trees, and soil yielding unusual, unpredictable crops? It's fine; stick 'em in some salads or brew 'em up for stew. Deserts infested with huge acid-spitting bugs? You could avoid them—or you could hunt them and use their spit to make alcohol. Sure, there were failed experiments. Many of them. But what we hear about today, beyond cautionary tales like "never eat skirath meat without cooking it thoroughly," are the successful ones, and the *most* successful ones are famous across Exandria. This is why you get folks from Wildemount who swear by a Marquesian cooking spice, and folks in Tal'Dorei whose favorite treat is a Marquesian cake.

And so we bring you the following recipes, successful experiments and worthwhile explorations all. Without leaving your kitchen, you can wander into the labyrinthine neighborhoods within the spires of Jrusar, delve into the jungles of the Oderan Wilds, traverse the markets and caravans of Ank'Harel, venture into the Rumedam Desert, or relax by the Bay of Gifts. Sample famous spices and infamous brews, try a strange new vegetable or two, or just make a fantastic sandwich. Whatever you choose, enjoy the journey, and be pleased.

Suncut Semolina Porridge with Dried Fig Compote

The western side of Ank'Harel is dominated by the flags, tents, and blankets of the Suncut Bazaar. The merchants of this huge open-air market number in the hundreds and are as varied as their wares, but many among them start their day with this hearty breakfast. The porridge itself comes together quickly, and the compote topping can (and should) be made well in advance. So you can eat fast, get to work, and have all the energy you need to tempt passersby before they empty their pockets gambling at the Luck's Run. Or, you know, whatever else you need energy for.

PREP TIME: 1 hour
COOK TIME: 30 minutes

___

Fig Compote

½ cup / 64g dried figs, medium diced

⅓ cup / 43g dried cherries

3 tablespoons dark brown sugar

2 star anise pods

1 cinnamon stick

⅓ cup / 80ml brandy

⅓ cup / 80ml hot water

*T*O MAKE THE FIG COMPOTE: One to 2 days before preparing the porridge, put the figs and cherries in a small bowl.

Add the brown sugar, star anise, cinnamon, brandy, and hot water to the bowl and stir until the fruit is fully coated with the liquid mixture. Make sure the figs and cherries are fully submerged in the liquid, then cover with plastic wrap. Allow the mixture to hydrate for 2 to 12 hours on your countertop, until the figs and cherries are plump and soft.

Set a small pot over medium heat and pour in the fig and cherry mixture. Stir until the mixture becomes viscous, 5 to 10 minutes. The mixture should coat the back of a spoon without dripping. Once thickened, remove from the heat and allow to cool.

Once the mixture is cool, remove the cinnamon stick and star anise pods and scoop the compote into a sterilized, sealable jar. It will keep, refrigerated, for up to 2 weeks.

recipe and ingredients continue ↪

Semolina Porridge

1 cup / 160g semolina

2½ cups / 590ml water

One 3.5-ounce / 113g can sweetened condensed milk

1 tablespoon orange blossom water

1 teaspoon vanilla bean powder

½ teaspoon kosher salt

2 or 3 pats of butter

1 cup / 240ml half-and-half

4 ounces / 115g chèvre (soft goat cheese), crumbled for garnish

⅓ cup / 43g roasted pistachios, roughly chopped for garnish

TO MAKE THE SEMOLINA PORRIDGE: In a medium pot, stir together the semolina, water, sweetened condensed milk, orange blossom water, vanilla bean powder, and salt until well combined.

Set the pot over medium-low heat and cook, stirring, until the porridge thickens to your liking, 3 to 7 minutes.

Turn down the heat to the lowest possible setting and stir in the butter pats and half-and-half until well incorporated and creamy, 2 to 3 minutes.

Divide the porridge among four bowls and top with the fig and cherry compote, chèvre, and pistachios. Serve immediately.

fownsee Hollow Breakfast Sandwich

In the center of Jrusar's Core Spire is Fownsee Hollow, a space hundreds of feet deep, ringed and crisscrossed by an array of ropes, ladders, and loose boards, each leading to one of a hundred tunnels. It is an intentionally confusing place. But if you know where you're going, you can find much of use, including some extremely tasty breakfast sandwiches. If you're not from there, we've spared you the search.* Here is the recipe for what we have been assured is the Hollow's finest breakfast sandwich, complete with all the fixings.

*And the inevitable attempt to overcharge you.**

**If you visit Fownsee Hollow, ask for the price of something, and are not dramatically overcharged, check your possessions: You are currently being pickpocketed.

PREP TIME: 25 minutes
COOK TIME: 40 minutes

———

1 medium red bell pepper

1½ teaspoons extra-virgin olive oil, plus 2 tablespoons

Kosher salt and freshly ground black pepper

1 small ripe avocado

⅓ cup / 80g mayonnaise

1 garlic clove, finely grated

1 tablespoon fresh lime juice

1 pound / 450g ground pork

3 tablespoons thinly sliced scallions (green and white parts)

2 tablespoons pure maple syrup

In a small or medium cast-iron skillet over medium-high heat, cook the whole red bell pepper until tender and deeply charred and blackened in spots, 15 to 25 minutes, turning the pepper as needed to ensure even charring on all sides (including the top and bottom of the pepper). The timing for this will vary greatly depending on the heat of your stovetop.

Transfer the bell pepper to a medium bowl, cover the top with plastic wrap, and let steam for 15 minutes. After the bell pepper is finished steaming, remove the stem, skin, and seeds, then slice into thin strips. Transfer the sliced bell pepper to a small bowl along with the 1½ teaspoons of olive oil and a pinch of salt and black pepper. Stir to combine and set aside.

Cut the avocado in half, remove the seed, and scoop the flesh into a miniature food processor. Add the mayonnaise, garlic, and lime juice. Season with salt and black pepper and blend until the mixture is very smooth. Transfer the avocado aioli to a small bowl, press plastic wrap directly onto the surface, and refrigerate until ready to use.

Preheat the oven to 275°F / 135°C. Line two baking sheets with parchment paper and set aside.

recipe and ingredients continue ☞

1½ teaspoons granulated garlic

1 teaspoon fennel seeds, lightly cracked

1 teaspoon dried rubbed sage

1 teaspoon onion powder

½ teaspoon crushed red pepper flakes

4 slices sharp Cheddar cheese

4 eggs

4 brioche hamburger buns, lightly toasted

NOTE: Store any leftover avocado aioli in the refrigerator for up to 5 days.

In a large bowl, combine the pork, scallions, maple syrup, granulated garlic, fennel seeds, sage, onion powder, red pepper flakes, and 2 teaspoons of salt. Mix with your hands until well combined. Divide the meat into four equal portions and form each into a 4-inch- / 10cm wide patty (about ½ inch thick). Transfer the formed patties to one of the prepared baking sheets. With your thumb, make a depression ¼ inch deep and 1 inch / 2.5cm wide in the center of each patty.

In a large nonstick skillet over medium-high heat, warm 1 tablespoon of the olive oil. When the oil starts to shimmer, add 2 sausage patties and cook until well-browned on the first side, about 5 minutes. Flip the patties and cook until browned on the second side and cooked through, 3 to 5 more minutes. Transfer the cooked patties to the second prepared baking sheet. Carefully wipe out the excess oil and any brown bits at the bottom of the skillet and add the remaining 1 tablespoon of oil. Cook the remaining 2 sausage patties and add to the baking sheet with the other cooked patties. Lower the heat under the skillet to medium (no need to clean out the skillet).

Top each sausage patty with a slice of Cheddar cheese and keep them warm in the oven while you cook the eggs.

Carefully crack the eggs into the skillet and cook until the whites are completely set but the yolks are still soft, 3 to 4 minutes. Season with salt and black pepper.

To assemble, spread a spoonful of the avocado aioli on each bottom half of the toasted brioche buns, then top with a cheese-topped sausage patty, roasted red bell pepper strips, and a fried egg. Spread more avocado aioli on each top half of the toasted brioche buns and place on top of the egg. Serve immediately.

Zhudanna's Welcome

While visiting the Core Spire in Jrusar, one of our researchers stayed briefly with an elderly lady named Zhudanna and was completely charmed by her and her cooking. Apparently some of her other tenants* keep bringing home extra hungry people with no notice. Once, she said, she ended up serving them the fruit she was boiling down for preserves. Yes, she called it "stew." And yes, they were very nice about it.** But she suspects it was too sweet, even with the cayenne. And that Laudna will never get the color back in her cheeks just eating fruit!*** Next time, Zhudanna will be ready. The fruit idea was a good start, but she's created a nice cold yogurt soup as a base and worked the cayenne into crisp wafer cookies. They'll love it! We certainly did.

Zhudanna spoke about them as if they might return at any moment, but she has only one guest room. We admit confusion.

**They're all such nice people, she would like us to stress. So lovely. Very hungry, don't keep regular hours, but so lovely!*

***Zhudanna considered this an important consideration, so we have faithfully included it even if we don't fully understand it.*

PREP TIME: 2 hours
COOK TIME: 30 minutes

Cold Yogurt Soup

2 egg yolks

⅓ cup / 65g granulated sugar

1 teaspoon vanilla bean powder

⅔ cup / 160g plain, full-fat Greek yogurt

4 cups / 950ml buttermilk

Zest and juice of 1 small lemon

Stewed Peaches

One 8.5-ounce / 240g can sliced peaches in syrup

1 tablespoon cornstarch

To make the cold yogurt soup: Several hours before serving, place the egg yolks, granulated sugar, and vanilla powder in a large bowl and mix, using an electric handheld mixer on high speed, until light and fluffy, about 3 minutes. Fold in the yogurt in batches.

Stir in the buttermilk and lemon zest and juice. Transfer the soup to a clean, sealable container and refrigerate for 2 to 24 hours.

To make the stewed peaches: In a small pot, add the peaches and syrup, reserving 2 to 3 tablespoons of syrup in a small bowl.

In the small bowl with the syrup, add the cornstarch and mix until well incorporated, making sure there are no lumps.

recipe and ingredients continue ☞

1 tablespoon light brown sugar

½ teaspoon ground nutmeg

Cinnamon and Cayenne Wafer Cookies

1 cup / 140g cornmeal

1 cup / 140g all-purpose flour

½ cup / 100g granulated sugar

1 tablespoon ground cinnamon

1 teaspoon cayenne pepper

½ teaspoon baking soda

½ teaspoon kosher salt

1 egg

½ cup (1 stick) / 113g unsalted butter, softened

1 teaspoon vanilla extract

Add the cornstarch mixture, brown sugar, and nutmeg to the peaches and heat on medium-low, stirring occasionally, for 5 to 7 minutes, until the peaches become viscous, like pie filling.

Transfer to a clean, sealable container and allow to cool to room temperature before refrigerating for 2 to 24 hours.

TO MAKE THE CINNAMON AND CAYENNE WAFER COOKIES: In a medium bowl, combine the cornmeal, flour, granulated sugar, cinnamon, cayenne, baking soda, and salt.

Make a well in the flour mixture, crack in the egg, and add the butter and vanilla extract. Stir vigorously until the dough forms a clumpy, sandy texture that sticks together, 2 to 3 minutes.

Place the dough on a sheet of parchment paper and roll into a log about 2 inches / 5cm in diameter and 8 to 9 inches / 20 to 23cm long. Refrigerate for 1 hour.

Preheat the oven to 350°F / 175°C and line a baking sheet with parchment paper. When the log is firm, use a sharp knife to cut it into twelve slices ½ inch to ¾ inch thick. Arrange on the prepared baking sheet about 1 inch / 2.5cm apart. Bake for 10 to 15 minutes, until golden brown. Remove from the oven and transfer to a rack to cool.

To serve, ladle 5 ounces / 150ml of the yogurt soup into each individual bowl and top with peaches and 2 or 3 cookies.

NOTES: The soup will keep for several days in the refrigerator.

Consuming raw eggs can be dangerous. Please use either shell eggs that have been treated to destroy Salmonella, by pasteurization or another approved method, or pasteurized egg products.

The Meat Man Hoagie

During the summer of 811 PD, word began to spread throughout Ank'Harel: a new crime lord was on the rise. Apart from his moniker—"the Meat Man"—little was known about him for sure. He was said to be a Marquesian human, but some pointed out strange shifts in his voice and demeanor, leading to a conspiracy theory that he went about disguised. Some said he sold fine art; some said he sold only fakes. But everyone agreed on this: Do not cross the Meat Man, because he holds a grudge, and he is creative about his revenge. In a transparent attempt to stay on his good side, some merchants began loudly praising the Meat Man.* One enterprising tavern keeper even went so far as to name a sandwich after him,** which we have recreated here.

*For instance, the boutique Ank'Harelian trading company Meatman Imports & Sexports is assumed to be an homage to the former crime lord. Some say that the actual Meat Man is involved, brazenly branding a legal, forward-facing company with his underworld moniker. We find this unlikely.

**Ironically, one of the swirling rumors was that the Meat Man ate no meat, so it is unknown if this attempt at flattery was successful. The tavern stayed open, free of stench clouds, and unattacked by ducks, so . . . probably?

PREP TIME: 10 minutes

———

3 tablespoons extra-virgin olive oil

3 tablespoons red wine vinegar

1 garlic clove, minced

1 teaspoon dried oregano

Kosher salt

¼ teaspoon freshly ground black pepper

Two 10-inch / 25cm hoagie or grinder rolls

2 tablespoons mayonnaise

In a small bowl, combine the olive oil, vinegar, garlic, oregano, ¼ teaspoon of salt, and the pepper. Whisk until emulsified and set aside.

Split each hoagie roll down the side lengthwise using a serrated knife. Spread a thin layer of mayonnaise on the top and bottom of the sandwich interiors. Add a thin, even layer of provolone cheese down the center of each roll. Top the cheese with an even layer of the prosciutto followed by layers of salami and mortadella. Top each sandwich with an even layer of sliced tomato and sprinkle with a pinch of salt. Top the tomato with a layer of sliced onion and peperoncini. Finish with a mound of shredded iceberg lettuce.

recipe and ingredients continue ☞

¼ pound / 115g thinly sliced provolone cheese (about 8 slices)

¼ pound / 115g thinly sliced prosciutto (about 8 slices; see Note)

¼ pound / 115g thinly sliced hard or Genoa salami (about 20 slices; see Note)

¼ pound / 115g thinly sliced mortadella (about 20 slices; see Note)

1 medium Roma tomato, thinly sliced (about 8 slices)

⅓ cup / 40g thinly sliced red onion (from about one-fourth of a small red onion)

¼ cup / 35g thinly sliced peperoncini, drained

1 cup / 72g thinly shredded iceberg lettuce (from about one-fourth of a head of lettuce)

Drizzle 3 tablespoons of the dressing evenly over the filling of each sandwich. Gently press the sandwiches down to compact them slightly, then cut them in half. If packing the sandwiches to go, wrap each in a layer of parchment or butcher paper and secure with a piece of tape.

NOTE: Feel free to use any deli meat in this sandwich; just make sure the total amount is roughly ¾ pound / 340g. Thinly sliced ham, olive loaf, and sandwich-style pepperoni would all work well.

Core Spire Street Meat

Don't want to stop browsing the markets of Jrusar's Core Spire to sit down for a meal? The food carts lining the streets offer some surprisingly fine fare in portable form, like these lamb lollipops with dipping sauce. Holding the lamb by the bone keeps your hands clean for your stroll through the emporium or your night rolling dice with friends.

PREP TIME: 6 hours
30 minutes
COOK TIME: 45 minutes

———

Red Wine Ketchup

¼ cup / 130g tomato paste

⅓ cup / 65g packed dark brown sugar

⅓ cup / 80ml apple cider vinegar

3 garlic cloves, minced

2 tablespoons Worcestershire sauce

1 tablespoon powdered mustard

1 teaspoon cayenne pepper

½ cup / 120ml Cabernet wine

Kosher salt and freshly ground black pepper

Lamb Lollies

1 full rack of lamb, cleaned and separated into lollies

⅓ cup / 80ml olive oil

2 tablespoons minced fresh rosemary

1 tablespoon minced fresh oregano

1 tablespoon dried mint

2 garlic cloves, minced

Kosher salt and freshly ground black pepper

TO MAKE THE RED WINE KETCHUP: In a medium pot over medium-low heat, add the tomato paste, brown sugar, apple cider vinegar, garlic, Worcestershire sauce, mustard, cayenne pepper, and wine and stir. Bring to a simmer, stirring occasionally to prevent scorching.

Once the ingredients have become fragrant and reduced by half, 20 to 30 minutes, remove from the heat and set aside to cool to room temperature. Season with salt and black pepper.

Place in a sterilized, sealable container and refrigerate for at least 4 hours and up to 24 hours.

TO MAKE THE LAMB LOLLIES: In a sealable container, drizzle the lamb with the olive oil and sprinkle on the rosemary, oregano, mint, and garlic. Turn and rub the lamb until it is thoroughly and evenly coated on all sides. Marinate in the refrigerator for 6 to 24 hours.

Heat a grill or plancha on high. Once hot, place the lollies on the grill. For a medium-rare lolly, cook on each side for about 2 minutes before flipping. Season with salt and black pepper. Flip the lollies and cook for an additional 2 minutes and season again.

Remove the lollies from the heat and let rest, covered, for 10 minutes before serving.

Serve with the ketchup.

NOTE: The ketchup can be refrigerated for up to 2 weeks.

Heartmoor Harvest

In the northwest corner of the Oderan Wilds, the ground becomes lower and wetter until the jungle begins to resemble a bog. In the Heartmoor, the plant life is lush even by jungle standards. Here thrive medicinal plants, strangely colored and twisted trees, carnivorous vines, beautifully glowing flowers, and human-sized, human-eating, mutated bog spiders. Only the brave, foolhardy, or desperate step off the Honored Trails into the tangle. There is one settlement, Heartmoor Hamlet, that has managed to take root in the midst of this odd wilderness. This salad uses crops like the ones this small village cultivates, while leaving out the more *dangerous* bits of flora—striking a balance between the familiar and strange, with blue potatoes and radishes, different textured greens, and a bright variety of colors.

PREP TIME: 25 minutes
COOK TIME: 25 minutes

——

1½ pounds / 680g small blue potatoes, scrubbed (see Notes)

½ cup / 120ml extra-virgin olive oil

Kosher salt and freshly ground black pepper

3 cups / 480g multicolored cherry tomatoes, halved

⅓ cup / 80ml white wine vinegar

1 small bunch radishes with nice green leafy tops (see Notes)

1 tablespoon Dijon mustard

2 teaspoons honey

Preheat the oven to 425°F / 220°C.

In a large bowl, combine the blue potatoes and 1 tablespoon of the olive oil. Season with salt and pepper, then spread the potatoes out on a small rimmed baking sheet (reserve the bowl). Roast in the oven until the potatoes are fork-tender, 20 to 25 minutes, stirring the potatoes once halfway through the cooking time. Let the potatoes cool slightly.

Meanwhile, in the same bowl that you used to season the potatoes, combine the cherry tomatoes, 2 tablespoons of the vinegar, and 2 tablespoons of the olive oil, and season with salt and pepper. Let marinate at room temperature while the potatoes roast, about 25 minutes, stirring occasionally.

Cut away the green tops from the radishes. Hand-tear the leaves into large pieces and set aside. Thinly slice half of the radishes and cut the other half into small wedges. Set aside, keeping the green tops and cut radishes separate.

recipe and ingredients continue ☞

½ cup / 10g fresh flat-leaf parsley leaves, lightly packed

1 cup / 15g torn fresh dill

1 ounce / 30g shaved Parmesan cheese (about ¾ cup)

2 cups / 40g baby arugula, lightly packed

Use a slotted spoon to scoop the marinated tomatoes into a medium bowl, then pour the marinade into a blender. Add one-fourth of the marinated tomatoes and the mustard, honey, and remaining 3 tablespoons plus 1 teaspoon of white wine vinegar. Season with salt and pepper and blend until smooth. Remove the cap from the blender lid and with the blender running at low speed, slowly drizzle in the remaining 5 tablespoons of olive oil. The dressing should have the consistency of a creamy vinaigrette that drizzles easily off the back of a spoon. If it is too thick, add a splash or two of water and blend it again.

In the same large bowl that the tomatoes were marinated in, combine the roasted potatoes, radish slices and wedges, and the remaining marinated tomatoes. Toss gently to combine. Reserve a bit of the parsley, dill, and Parmesan cheese to use for a garnish, then add the rest to the bowl along with the baby arugula and radish greens. Season with salt and pepper and gently toss to combine. Transfer half of the salad to a large platter and drizzle with some of the tomato vinaigrette. Top with the remaining salad and drizzle with more of the tomato vinaigrette. Garnish with the reserved parsley, dill, and Parmesan. Serve immediately with any extra vinaigrette on the side.

NOTES: Small blue potatoes work well in this salad because they resemble small stones, but you can substitute red-skinned or baby Yukon Gold potatoes if needed. If your potatoes are on the larger side, slice them in half before you roast them.

If your radishes do not have nice green leafy tops, you can substitute 1½ cups / 30g of additional baby arugula instead.

If you have any leftover vinaigrette, transfer it to an airtight container and store in the refrigerator for up to 5 days.

Muffins of the Shadow Baker

The Lantern Spire is the first stop for many visitors to Jrusar, being the only way into the city on foot. Once there, you'll find crowded streets winding up and around the spire toward the ever-burning light of the Prakash Pyre that gives the spire its name. If you ignore those streets, though, and find a way inside the spire, you could find yourself at the Elder's Post grey market.* If you are lucky, you might come across Ephred, the master pastry chef known as the Shadow Baker. And if you are very lucky, the pockets of his cloak might still contain some delightful treats to buy.

Few among us are so lucky,** so we have attempted to re-create two of the Shadow Baker's muffins for the home cook. Beginning with the same batter, they then diverge into savory and sweet options. The savory muffin has sausage and potato, while the sweet is topped with cinnamon sugar crumble and served with the Shadow Baker's signature blackberry citrus butter.

*You could also find yourself extremely disoriented or extremely robbed. Proceed with caution.
**But if you are, please say hi for us! We are big Shadow Baker fans here at Exquisite Exandria.

recipe continues ☞

Conciliatory Couscous

After you've become accustomed to eating animal products, it can be hard to break the habit. Even if, for instance, you're trying to placate a vegan relative who complains about how much chicken you eat, sometimes you're not sure what to eat instead. May we recommend this couscous, inspired by the caravan cookpots of Ank'Harel's River District. The base is vegetable stock, the additions are a colorful concoction of tomatoes, olives, lemons, herbs, and spice. And then, right at the end, you drizzle a bunch of butter over the top. Look, she knows you're doing your best.

PREP TIME: 20 minutes
COOK TIME: 30 minutes

—

½ cup (1 stick) / 113g butter

2 cups / 320g dried couscous

2 cups / 475ml hot vegetable stock

⅓ cup / 20g dry sun-dried tomatoes, roughly chopped

⅓ cup / 55g pitted green olives, drained, and roughly chopped

1 preserved lemon with rind, small diced

½ cup / 64g parsley, chopped

1½ teaspoons ground cinnamon

2 sprigs mint, torn

Kosher salt and freshly ground black pepper

In a small saucepan over medium-high heat, melt the butter and cook until it begins to brown, 3 to 5 minutes. The butter will begin to accumulate white froth around its edges and turn a walnut color. Once browned, remove from the heat and set aside.

In a large bowl, combine the couscous, hot vegetable stock, and sun-dried tomatoes. Cover with plastic wrap and set aside to hydrate for 15 to 20 minutes.

Once hydrated, drizzle in the brown butter and fluff the couscous with a fork.

Toss with the olives, preserved lemon, parsley, cinnamon, and mint. Season with salt and pepper.

Spire by Fire's Beer-Braised Brisket

• MAKES 6 TO 8 SERVINGS •

The Spire by Fire is a huge, labyrinthine tavern built into the side of the Core Spire in Jrusar. The owners used the natural contours of the spire creatively, building in and around and through until the tavern attained six stories and enough renown to do business at all hours of the day and night. That spirit of creative efficiency reaches every aspect of the business, including the menu, which owner Ishir has been tweaking for the last decade. His latest innovation is this beer-braised brisket. It serves at least half a dozen people, is cooked mostly by throwing it into an oven and leaving it alone, and uses up the beer dregs that accumulate throughout the evening.*

We suspect he may have told us that last part in confidence. He was a little drunk at the time. But on the other hand, he knew we were writing a cookbook. So, a compromise: If you happen to be in the Spire by Fire, don't tell anyone where the leftover beer goes.

PREP TIME: 20 minutes
COOK TIME: 4 hours 30 minutes

___

2 tablespoons light brown sugar

Kosher salt and freshly ground black pepper

1 teaspoon garlic powder

1 teaspoon paprika, preferably smoked

One 4-pound / 1.8kg untrimmed flat-cut beef brisket

3 tablespoons vegetable oil

1½ cups / 210g diced yellow onion (from about 1 large onion)

3 large celery ribs, cut into 1½-inch / 2.5cm chunks (about 2 cups / 150g)

In a small bowl, mix together the brown sugar, 2 teaspoons of salt, 1 teaspoon of pepper, the garlic powder, and paprika. Pat the brisket dry with paper towels and rub the spice mixture evenly over the entire surface. Transfer to a large plate or baking sheet and refrigerate for at least 30 minutes and up to overnight.

Set a rack in the middle of the oven and preheat to 300°F / 150°C. In a large Dutch oven or oven-safe heavy-bottomed pot with a lid, heat the vegetable oil over medium-high heat until it shimmers. Add the brisket and sear until dark brown, 4 to 6 minutes. (It's okay if the brisket is slightly too large for the pot and the edges come up the sides; it will shrink while cooking.) Flip the brisket and sear on the other side until dark brown, 4 to 6 minutes. Transfer the brisket to a large plate and set aside.

recipe and ingredients continue ☞

2 large carrots, peeled, halved, and cut into 1-inch / 2.5cm chunks (about 2 cups / 230g)

5 garlic cloves, minced

2 teaspoons chopped fresh rosemary leaves (from about 2 sprigs)

2 teaspoons chopped fresh thyme leaves (from about 10 sprigs)

24 ounces / 710ml beer such as porter, stout, or pale ale (see Note)

2 cups / 475ml unsalted beef stock

One 28-ounce / 794g can crushed tomatoes

2 dried bay leaves

Crusty bread, mashed potatoes, or polenta, for serving (optional)

Add the onion to the pot and continue cooking over medium-high heat, stirring often, until lightly browned and softened, 4 to 6 minutes. Add the celery, carrots, garlic, rosemary, and thyme and continue cooking, stirring often, until very fragrant, 1 to 2 minutes. Add the beer, beef stock, and crushed tomatoes and stir together while scraping the bottom of the pot to loosen any brown bits. Return the brisket to the pot, fat side up, and nestle it into the vegetables. Add the bay leaves, cover with a lid, and carefully transfer to the oven. Cook until the meat can easily be torn apart with a fork, 3 to 3½ hours. If the meat still feels tough, cook for an additional 30 minutes and check it again.

Transfer the brisket to a large cutting board and tent with foil. Strain the braising liquid through a fine-mesh strainer and discard the solids. Return the strained braising liquid to the pot and bring to a boil over high heat. Cook, stirring occasionally, until the sauce has thickened and reduced by about half, 15 to 20 minutes. Season with salt and pepper.

Thinly slice the brisket against the grain and arrange on a large serving platter. Top the brisket with a few ladles of the braising liquid and serve the remainder on the side. Serve with crusty bread, mashed potatoes, or polenta, if desired.

NOTE: Just about any beer can be used in this recipe. Pale ales will provide a brighter, more hoppy flavor, while darker beers like stouts will give the sauce a richer, more gravy-like flavor. Just avoid using any flavored beers or beers brewed with fruit.

"Meal"

A hidden gem awaits travelers to the industrial Smolder Spire in Jrusar. Working at the Soot and Swill tavern, an unassuming working-class establishment, is a chef named Pretty. Pretty is an ogre of stunning depth, focus, and culture, and he uses all three to make just one thing. That thing is the dinner he simply, humbly calls "Meal."

Do not be fooled by the monotone coloration on the plate! That is merely the gravy, and it is but the wrapping for the fine present that has been created for you. Dig in, and you'll find layers of delightful surprises: spiced ham, thick baked beans, even entire oranges await you.

You can, we suppose, serve the gravy on the side. You can also, we further suppose, not allow it to congeal before serving. But do not, we beg you, tell Pretty of your wanton disregard for his art! At least, not without a Drink* in his hand.

*Pretty's beverage of choice. We could not get anyone to tell us what's in it, since, we're assuming, its boldness would shock normal palates.**

**Our attempts to re-create Drink in our test kitchen were unsuccessful. The closest contender was a random mix of hard liquor plus an entire jar of olive juice. But that can't be right.

PREP TIME: 30 minutes
COOK TIME: 5 hours
10 minutes

——

Ham

One 8- to 10-pound /
3.6 to 4.5kg whole
bone-in smoked dinner
ham, unsliced

3 cups / 710ml water

1 teaspoon whole cloves

3 cinnamon sticks

2 star anise pods

3 navel oranges or
5 mandarin oranges

⅓ cup / 80ml pulp-free
orange juice

*T*O PREPARE THE HAM: Remove the ham from the refrigerator and use a sharp knife to score any fat at the top of the ham in a 1-inch / 2.5cm diamond pattern. Let the ham sit at room temperature for 30 minutes. Preheat the oven to 350°F / 175°C, and if you plan to bake the ham and beans simultaneously, place one rack on the bottom for the ham, and the second rack at the top for the beans.

In a large roasting pan, combine the water, cloves, cinnamon sticks, and star anise. Peel the oranges, leaving them whole (reserve for the gravy). Tear any of the larger pieces of orange peel into smaller pieces so that they will be submerged in the water, and add the peels and pith to the roasting pan with the water and spices.

recipe and ingredients continue ↬

fusaka

Fusaka is a Marquesian cooking spice so popular that its fans are found as far away as the Menagerie Coast in Wildemount. It is, however, not readily available outside those regions. The flavor is specific: a little meaty, a little cheesy, a little zesty. It's hard to explain and even harder to re-create. But we are proud to say that we have, at least, accomplished the latter. Here is a mix that will approximate this beloved spice and is appropriate for sprinkling over meat, vegetables, fish, or even popcorn.*

Do not, under any circumstances, attempt to insert fusaka into your nonmouth orifices in any manner for any reason. We can't believe we even have to write this.

PREP TIME: 5 minutes

½ cup / 64g brewer's yeast

2 tablespoons dried cilantro

1 tablespoon dried dill

1 tablespoon garlic powder

½ tablespoon mastic gum, ground into a powder

1 tablespoon smoked sea salt

½ tablespoon dried lemon or orange peel powder

1 tablespoon MSG (optional)

Combine the brewer's yeast, cilantro, dill, garlic powder, mastic gum, smoked sea salt, lemon powder, and MSG (if desired) in a medium bowl. Transfer to a sealable jar and store for up to 1 month in a cool, dry place.

Use fusaka seasoning to sprinkle over popcorn, meat, fish, or vegetables.

Adra's Magical Flavored Ice

When the month of Sydenstar has come, and the long, hot days are wearing you down, perk up your taste buds with this icy treat. Developed by an Ank'Harelian street magician named Adra to encourage attendance at their performances, the Magical Flavored Ice soon became more popular than the magic. After decades of success, Adra has decided to retire. So here, for the first time, they have graciously agreed to share their secret recipe. Since many home cooks will be unable to procure ripe Marquesian kurrak, Adra assures us that jackfruit is an excellent alternative topping.

PREP TIME: 15 minutes
**COOK TIME: 1 hour
35 minutes**

———

**One 13.5- to 14-ounce /
380 to 400ml can full-fat
coconut milk, well shaken**

**1 cup / 200g granulated
sugar**

Kosher salt

Zest of 1 large lime

**⅓ cup / 20g sweetened
shredded coconut**

6 cups / 1.4L water

**1 pound / 450g purple
yams, peeled and cut into
¾-inch chunks**

4 cups / 600g ice cubes

**6 ounces / 170g drained
canned jackfruit in syrup,
sliced into thin strips
(about 1 cup; see Notes)**

**1 pound / 454g frozen
unsweetened young
coconut strips, thawed
and well drained
(see Notes)**

In a medium saucepan over medium heat, combine the coconut milk, ½ cup / 100g of the sugar, and ¼ teaspoon salt. Whisk until the mixture is well combined and smooth. Bring the mixture to a gentle simmer, about 10 minutes, stirring frequently and scraping down the sides of the saucepan occasionally. Continue to cook, stirring occasionally and adjusting the heat as needed to maintain a gentle simmer, until the mixture is reduced by about half (to about 1 cup / 240ml) and thickened to a consistency similar to cream of coconut (the color will also go from milky white to more of a translucent pale gray), about 1 hour. Transfer the sweetened condensed coconut milk into a small bowl, cool completely, then stir in the lime zest. Set aside.

Preheat the oven to 325°F / 165°C. Spread the sweetened shredded coconut out in a single layer on a small baking sheet. Bake until well toasted and golden brown throughout, about 10 minutes, stirring occasionally to prevent the coconut from burning. Transfer to a small bowl and set aside.

Line a large plate with a couple of paper towels and set aside. In a large saucepan, combine the water, the remaining ½ cup / 100g sugar, and the purple yam chunks. Bring to a boil over high heat, stirring occasionally, about 10 minutes. Once at a boil, stir in 2 teaspoons of salt, lower the heat to a strong simmer, and cook until the yam chunks are fork-tender but still hold their shape, about 5 more minutes. Use a slotted spoon to transfer the yam to the prepared plate and arrange the yam chunks in a single layer. Set aside to cool completely.

When you are ready to serve, working in batches, pulse the ice cubes in a food processor until the ice is crushed into very fine pieces similar to shave ice. Divide the ice among four tall glasses, then layer with a good drizzle of the sweetened condensed coconut milk (2 to 3 tablespoons per glass), the sliced jackfruit, thawed unsweetened coconut strips, cooked purple yam chunks, and another drizzle of sweetened condensed coconut milk (about 1 tablespoon per glass). Sprinkle with the toasted shredded coconut and serve immediately.

NOTES: We use canned jackfruit in this recipe because it can be easier to source than fresh jackfruit, but if you are able to find the fresh version, do use it here.

If you can find only frozen sweetened young coconut strips (also sometimes called coconut meat slices or sliced young coconut), you can still use it, but make sure to give it a good rinse to remove the excess sugar.

Store any leftover sweetened condensed coconut milk in an airtight container and store in the refrigerator for up to 14 days. To use, warm it ever so slightly in the microwave or on the stovetop until it loosens up just enough to easily drizzle off of a spoon.

Pike's Purple Jewel Cake of Marquet

"There once lived a woman named Madame Marquita Parcata," begins the old tale. Madame Parcata gave a tired, thirsty girl water, but refused to give her shelter. When the little girl offered to grant a wish in return, Madame Parcata made an ill-advised choice, wishing to have great fame and worth. As payment in kind for her inhospitable greed, she was turned into a huge purple jewel, as big as an apple. This is the story behind the delicacy known as the Purple Jewel Cake of Marquet, beloved by people across Exandria, including Vox Machina's Pike Trickfoot. The story changes depending on the teller, but all agree on two things: the part about the apple is important, and the cake is delicious.

PREP TIME: 20 minutes
COOK TIME: 50 minutes

———

2.4 ounces / 68g freeze-dried blueberries (about 1½ cups)

1⅓ cups / 185g all-purpose flour

1 teaspoon baking powder

Kosher salt

½ cup (1 stick) / 110g unsalted butter, at room temperature

¾ cup / 150g granulated sugar

3 egg whites, at room temperature

¾ cup / 175g unsweetened applesauce, at room temperature

1 teaspoon vanilla extract

1½ tablespoons white sparkling sugar

Preheat the oven to 350°F / 175°C. Lightly grease an 8½ by 4½-inch / 22 by 11cm loaf pan with nonstick cooking spray and set aside. Place a fine-mesh strainer over a medium bowl and set aside.

In batches, grind the freeze-dried blueberries until broken down into a fine powder. Transfer to the fine-mesh strainer and use the back of a spoon or rubber spatula to push the powder through the strainer and into the bowl (discard any seeds). Add the flour, baking powder, and ¾ teaspoon of salt and whisk until well combined and there are no clumps of the ground berries left in the mixture. Set aside.

In a large bowl, combine the butter and granulated sugar. Use an electric handheld mixer to blend on low speed at first to incorporate the ingredients, then on medium-high until the mixture is light and fluffy, about 5 minutes, scraping down the bowl as needed. Add the egg whites, one-third at a time, beating well and scraping down the sides of the bowl after each addition. Add half of the flour mixture and blend on low speed until almost combined. Add the applesauce and vanilla extract and blend until mostly combined, then add the remaining flour mixture and blend until the batter is starting to come together. Switch over to a rubber spatula and gently stir the batter by hand until smooth and combined. You do

recipe continues ☞

Using a 1½-inch / 4cm cookie scoop (or two rounded tablespoons), portion out the dough and roll into balls. Roll the balls in the turbinado sugar and place at least 3 inches / 7.5cm apart on the prepared baking sheets (8 per tray).

Bake two pans at the same time, swapping the top sheet to the bottom rack and bottom sheet to the top midway through baking, until the tops crack and the cookies are lightly browned around the edges, 13 to 14 minutes. Bake the remaining tray on either rack. (If reusing one of the baking sheets, let it cool for at least 15 minutes before reusing.) Let cool completely on the baking sheets.

Sandkheg Hide Ale

Sandkhegs are eight-foot-long armored insects with acidic spit to poison their prey, hooked front legs to grab it, and strong mandibles to bite it in half. Despite this description, some folks venture out into the Rumedam Desert, collect the spit, and make it into alcohol. The resulting spirit numbs the drinker's throat so completely that they often can't speak. In short, the liquor known as Sandkheg's Hide is the result of an absolutely wild series of life choices. We recommend that you make this home version instead, and then cut it with ale.

PREP TIME: 20 minutes

Szechuan Dry Gin

¼ cup / 32g Szechuan peppercorns

8 ounces / 240ml London dry gin

Ice cubes, for serving

12 ounces / 360ml pink grapefruit juice

8 ounces / 240ml Belgian-style pale ale

Elderflower bitters, to taste

*T*O MAKE THE SZECHUAN DRY GIN: In a sterilized, sealable jar, add the peppercorns and gin. Seal the lid tightly and store the jar in a cool, dark place for about 1 week. Strain with a small sieve before using to prevent peppercorns from getting into the drink.

In a 4 to 6 ounce glass filled with ice, combine 1 to 2 ounces / 30 to 60ml of Szechuan gin, 3 ounces / 90ml of grapefruit juice, and 2 ounces / 60ml of pale ale. Finish with 2 or 3 dashes of elderflower bitters per glass. Stir and serve.

Dalen's Closet Special

In the northern port city of Shammel, the once sleepy resort called Dalen's Closet has enjoyed a consistent uptick in business since it hosted the wedding of Vex'ahlia and Percival de Rolo in 813 PD. The Closet, as owner Guath refers to it, is famous for its beautiful beaches, its near-endless rows of hammocks, and its fruity drinks. While we can't bring you beaches or hammocks, we can at least evoke the feeling of those breezy, bright, sleepy days with this delicious sangria. Guath has added dragon fruit in a cheeky nod to Vox Machina's monster-slaying days, but we've included substitutions in case dragon fruit isn't available to you.

PREP TIME: 4 hours 15 minutes

———

1½ cups / 360ml unsweetened pineapple juice

1 cup / 240ml passionfruit or guava juice

¼ cup / 50g granulated sugar

¼ cup / 60ml fresh lime juice plus 1 large lime, sliced into thin rounds

One 750ml bottle crisp white wine (such as Sauvignon Blanc)

4 ounces / 120ml coconut rum

1 large ripe mango, peeled and cut into large chunks

½ large ripe pineapple, peeled, cored, and cut into large chunks

1 large pink dragon fruit (see Note)

Ice cubes, for serving

In an extra-large pitcher or bowl, combine the pineapple juice, passionfruit or guava juice, sugar, and lime juice. Stir until the sugar is completely dissolved. Add the lime slices, white wine, coconut rum, mango, and pineapple. Stir to combine and refrigerate the sangria for at least 4 hours and up to overnight.

Meanwhile, cut the dragon fruit in half lengthwise. Slice one half into six to eight equal pieces (they will look similar to half-moons) and arrange in a single layer on a large plate. Use a large spoon to scoop out the flesh from the other half of the fruit, then cut the flesh into ½-inch pieces. Transfer to a small bowl and refrigerate the dragon fruit until ready to serve.

Fill six to eight large wineglasses halfway with ice cubes, then pour the sangria evenly into the glasses (making sure that everyone gets a good helping of the fruit). Sprinkle some of the chopped dragon fruit on top of the sangria in each glass. Cut a small slit into each slice of dragon fruit and place one on the rim of each glass along with a small paper cocktail umbrella. Serve immediately.

NOTE: You can substitute 3 or 4 kiwis or 2 cups / 240g of strawberries in place of the dragon fruit.

4
WILDEMOUNT

WILDEMOUNT

Finally, we travel back the way we came, north and east over the Lucidian Ocean to Tal'Dorei, and then past it, across the Ozmit Sea, to Wildemount. Wildemount is a continent that, in the best of times, thrives on its interconnectedness. This has huge appeal to us, of course, because one of the many magical things about food is its ability to bring people together. But before we can expand on that theme, we need to set the table, as it were, by skimming briefly back through some of Wildemount's worst, most divided times.

We'll start with the continent's most literal divide: the Ashkeeper Peaks. East of the Peaks is Xhorhas, the land that saw the bitter end of the Calamity. Here, the Prime Deities brought the fight to Ghor Dranas, the city of the Betrayer Gods. By the time the fighting was done, Ghor Dranas was in ruins, and the land for miles around was cursed, poisoned, and infested with monstrosities. Yet from this destruction came an unexpected ray of hope, a literal light in the darkness. A society of elves living deep under Ghor Dranas, inspired by a deity they called the Luxon, made their way to the surface and claimed the ruins as their own. The house, or den, of Kryn united the other families under their name, founding the Kryn Dynasty that endures to this day with the aptly named Rosohna, or "Rebirth," as its capital city. Strong magic allows the elves to cast the city in perpetual night, shielding their eyes from the full strength of the sun. That magic is one of many ever-present reminders of how different the Dynasty is from the rest of Wildemount, and rumor and superstition still thrive centuries later. Outside of Xhorhas, in fact, many insist on calling Rosohna "Ghor Dranas" to this day.

Among those who assumed ill intent of the Kryn were the rulers of the Dwendalian Empire, the neighboring power that controls much of the land west of the Ashkeepers. In a throwback to the beliefs that sparked the Calamity, the Dwendalian kings have declared that divine magic and most religious worship are trickery and deceit. The Kryn's worship of the Luxon, therefore, is considered deeply threatening. Most recently, the Cerberus Assembly, the powerful mage faction that advises the throne, joined King Bertrand Dwendal in proclaiming that the Dynasty had evil designs on Empire lands. The fear this stoked helped king and assembly keep the people of the Empire under totalitarian control for decades.

When two of the Luxon beacons, the Kryn's most precious artifacts, went missing, the Kryn sent two soldiers to the Empire city of Zadash to attempt their recovery. The attempt went bad, the Empire declared war, armies deployed from both sides, and the well-being of the people of Wildemount teetered in the balance.

But less than a year later, the war between the Kryn Dynasty and the Dwendalian Empire was over. A group of adventurers known as the Mighty Nein had succeeded in brokering talks between the two peoples. The beacons were found and returned, political prisoners were exchanged, and an uneasy peace was declared. Two months later, again spurred by the Mighty Nein, the Cobalt Soul opened investigations into evildoing by the mage Trent Ikithon and the Assembly.

In the span of a season, this motley group of friends had stopped a war and felled a pillar of corruption at the heart of a totalitarian government. They had tipped the balance of a continent from aggression to cooperation, from division to connection. Their deeds aren't as well documented as those of Vox Machina, but word has trickled in from across Wildemount that the Nein aren't merely diplomats or spies. They rescued a small town from a harmful cult, killed a group

of slavers, and closed dangerous abyssal rifts beneath the city of Asarius, to name but a few of their heroic acts. They've been as far south as Darktow, where they were seen conversing with the Plank King, and as far north as Uthodurn in the Flotket Alps. They were even rumored to be exploring frigid Eiselcross, searching for the ruined flying city of Aeor. They've got members from the Empire, from southern Xhorhas, from the neutral Menagerie Coast, from the lawless Greying Wildlands, and possibly from the Kryn Dynasty itself. So who are they, really?

There's Caleb Widogast, rumored to be Trent Ikithon's former student—a mage who can manipulate gravity, command flame, and create invisible towers, who was often seen in the company of his magical cat, Frumpkin. Beauregard Lionett—a hand-to-hand fighter from the Empire town of Kamordah and expositor of the Cobalt Soul—is also the heir of a successful wine family. Yasha Nydoorin is a fierce brawler from south Xhorhas, a devotee of the Stormlord, and Beau's partner. Jester Lavorre, the healer from Nicodranas on the Menagerie Coast, has a famous sweet tooth and is the daughter of the renowned courtesan known as the Ruby of the Sea. Fjord Stone, an accomplished sailor from the Menagerie Coast who now fights in the Wildmother's name, is also Jester's partner and a rumored one-time pirate captain. Veth Brenatto, known for a time as Nott the Brave, uses her thief's skill set, deadly crossbow, and tricky magic to protect the ones she loves, including her husband and son. Caduceus Clay, healer of the Wildmother, joined the group from the Savalirwood in the Greying Wildlands, and his comforting presence and healing touch kept everyone alive more than once. The Mighty Nein have also been seen with a colorful horned swordsman and, on a few occasions, with Essek Thelyss, a mage high in the Kryn Dynasty's pecking order. Counting those two would bring us to a very satisfying total of nine, but since "Mighty Nein" just means "Big No," we suspect that's a coincidence.

In any case, the Mighty Nein represents the best of Wildemount culture: a huge range of people, side by side, who lose none of their uniqueness. All these lands, all these cultures, exist next to each other across the continent. The militaristic, rule-bound Empire; the striving, driven Dynasty; the fiercely independent Menagerie Coast; and the wild lands that surround them can, and should, continue to salute and respect each other.

And so we've taken our cue from the Nein and brought you a range of dishes from north, south, east, and west: a drink from Deastok next to one from Aeor, meat pies from Xhorhas next to mushroom toast from the Savalirwood. Sweet and savory, vegetarian and meat-loving, heavy and light, alcohol-free and so-alcoholic-it-might-actually-explode. Do we need to fight over which one is right, which one is best? *Nein*.

Nestled Nook Breakfast Special

Near the southern tip of the Marrow Valley lies the Empire town of Trostenwald. The rare varieties of wheat and other grains grown only in this area yield a delectable array of sweet ales, known as trosts. These trosts are the main draw of Trostenwald, providing a brisk export trade and tempting travelers coming north from Nicodranas or south from Zadash to draw out their rest stops before continuing on their road.

For those travelers who get too deep in their cups, there are always inns like the Nestled Nook. Innkeeper Yorda will set you up with a warm bed for the night and a warm breakfast in the morning (or whenever you manage to get downstairs). Yorda has a range of foods on offer, but it's the meat selection that really sets the Nestled Nook apart. We've recreated two of her most popular dishes here: brats and bacon. Note how they both meet a need that less experienced innkeepers might overlook: namely, portability. The brat comes in a convenient bun, so we'd suggest eating that one first. You can stick the bacon in your pocket for later.

recipe continues ☞

Pocket Bacon

PREP TIME: 10 minutes
COOK TIME: 20 minutes

---

8 strips slab bacon

¼ cup / 60ml maple syrup

3 tablespoons apple cider vinegar

½ teaspoon smoked paprika

2 tablespoons coarsely ground black pepper

Preheat the oven to 400°F / 200°C, and line a rimmed baking sheet with parchment paper. Top the baking sheet with a wire rack.

Place the bacon on the rack and bake for 10 to 12 minutes, until the bacon is mostly cooked.

While the bacon is cooking, in a small bowl, mix together the maple syrup, apple cider vinegar, and smoked paprika.

At the 10- to 12-minute mark, pull the bacon out and glaze on one side with the maple syrup mixture. Sprinkle pepper over each strip and cook until the glaze is sticky, 8 to 10 minutes.

Stick these in your pocket to eat for later.

Breakfast Beer Brats

PREP TIME: 35 minutes
COOK TIME: 20 minutes

---

8 uncooked bratwurst links

24 ounces / 710ml your favorite milk stout beer

½ cup / 120ml water

Compound Butter

¼ cup (½ stick) / 55g butter, room temperature

2 tablespoons maple syrup

1 teaspoon ground cinnamon

¼ teaspoon ground nutmeg

Apple Slaw

1 medium Honeycrisp, Jonagold, or Braeburn apple, cored and julienned

1 medium Granny Smith apple, cored and julienned

1 cup / 50g shredded red or green cabbage

¼ cup / 60ml apple cider vinegar

1 small red onion, thinly sliced

Kosher salt and freshly ground black pepper

8 brioche hot dog buns

At least 4 to 6 hours before grilling, marinate the brats in the milk stout and water. Cover and refrigerate.

TO MAKE THE COMPOUND BUTTER: In a small bowl, use a silicone spatula to fold together the butter, maple syrup, cinnamon, and nutmeg until well incorporated. Set aside.

Preheat the grill or plancha on high to at least 400°F / 200°C.

In a large pot, add the brats and beer liquid and heat on high until the liquid is boiling. Lower the heat to a simmer and cook for 20 minutes, or until the brat temperature reaches at least 145°F / 63°C and holds for 4 seconds.

TO MAKE THE APPLE SLAW: In a small bowl, combine the apples, cabbage, apple cider vinegar, and onion. Season with salt and pepper and set aside.

While the brats are simmering, evenly butter the insides of the hot dog buns—both sides—with the compound butter and set aside.

When the brats are done simmering, place them on the grill or plancha and grill for 1 to 3 minutes before flipping. The brats should be toasty brown with visible grill marks. Once flipped, cook for an additional 1 to 3 minutes.

One minute before the brats are ready to be pulled from the grill or plancha, place the hot dog buns, buttered sides down, on the grill and allow to toast until crispy and slightly golden, 30 seconds to 1 minute.

To serve, place the brats in the buns, top with apple slaw, and enjoy!

Jester's Sweet Feast

Most have heard tell of a wondrous magical banquet that calms the mind, cures the body, and invigorates the spirit. But few have had the honor of seeing, never mind partaking in, a feast the way Jester Lavorre does it. While she casts this complex spell, she manages to take any requests her diners throw her way—from candied bugs to "please, gods, just one vegetable" —and incorporate them into a beautifully plated spread that delights all the senses. But no matter the season, the country, or the time of day, one thing makes its way into all of Jester's feasts: pastries.

Now, even narrowing our focus to pastries, we don't have the space to discuss everything Jester has created. So we've limited ourselves to three offerings, all of which use the same dough as a base. To satisfy your sweet tooth, try the plum Danishes. For something sweet with that Nicodranas cinnamon kick, there are spiced muffins with cherry jam. And if you prefer savory, there are salt-and-pepper cheese twists.*

Jester puts some dipping honey on the side for when you come to your senses.

recipe continues ☞

Rough Puff Pastry Dough

PREP TIME: 3 hours

___

2 cups / 280g all-purpose flour, plus more for dusting

1 tablespoon granulated sugar

2½ teaspoons kosher salt

¾ cup (1½ sticks) / 165g cold unsalted butter, cut crosswise into ¼-inch-thick slices

¼ cup / 60ml cold buttermilk

4 to 6 tablespoons / 60 to 90ml ice water

In a large bowl, stir together the flour, sugar, and salt. Add the butter slices, tossing them through the flour until each individual piece is well coated. Cut the butter into the flour by pressing and breaking the pieces between your fingers until each slice is broken down into 2 or 3 large pieces. As you work, continue to toss the butter with the flour so that the new broken pieces are recoated in the flour.

Drizzle the buttermilk on top of the flour mixture and use your hands to toss the flour with the buttermilk. The mixture will still be fairly dry at this point. Add the ice water, 1 tablespoon at a time, using your hands to stir the water into the flour and butter at first then lightly kneading as the dough starts to come together more. Stop kneading when the mixture comes together to form a shaggy dough with large pieces of butter throughout. It should hold together when you hold a clump of the dough in the palm of your hand, but the dough should not be at all wet. Form the dough into a rectangle 1 inch / 2.5cm thick. Wrap tightly in plastic wrap and refrigerate until the dough is firm and the large pieces of butter are completely chilled again (they will have warmed up a bit as you worked the dough), about 1 hour.

Lightly dust a clean work surface with flour, then top with the dough. Lightly dust a rolling pin and roll the dough out into an 8 by 12-inch / 20 by 30cm rectangle about ¼ inch thick. Bring the two shorter sides together so that the two ends meet in the center, then gently fold the two ends together again. Turn the dough so the longest side is facing you and roll the dough out into the same size rectangle and fold again. This counts as two folds. Wrap the dough tightly in plastic wrap and chill until the dough is mostly firm, about 30 minutes.

Lightly dust the work surface again and repeat the rolling and folding process two additional times for a total of four folds. As you roll and fold the dough, the butter pieces will get smaller and smaller. By the last fold, you should no longer be able to see any visible pieces of butter and the dough should be smooth.

Once the final fold is completed, wrap the dough tightly in plastic wrap and refrigerate for at least 1 hour before using, or freeze for up to 3 months.

Roasted Plum Danishes

PREP TIME: 1 hour 30 minutes
COOK TIME: 30 minutes

———

2 tablespoons unsalted butter, sliced into 4 pieces

3 tablespoons light brown sugar

Kosher salt

4 large ripe red plums, halved and pitted

1 egg yolk, at room temperature

4 ounces / 115g cream cheese, at room temperature

3 tablespoons confectioners' sugar, plus more for dusting

1 teaspoon vanilla extract

1 sheet Rough Puff Pastry Dough (page 160), chilled

All-purpose flour, for dusting

Preheat the oven to 400°F / 200°C.

In an 8-inch / 20cm baking dish, scatter the butter pieces and place in the hot oven until the butter is just melted, about 2 minutes. Remove the baking dish from the oven, sprinkle the brown sugar and a pinch of salt over the butter, and stir to combine (the mixture will not be smooth, but the brown sugar will melt slightly into the butter). Add the plums and stir the plums to coat in the butter mixture, then turn the plums so they are all cut side down. Roast until the plums are tender but still hold their shape, about 25 minutes, brushing the tops of the plums with the butter sauce after 15 minutes. Remove from the oven and cool the plums completely in the butter sauce. Turn off the oven.

Line two large baking sheets with parchment paper and set aside.

Line a large plate with several paper towels, then use a slotted spatula to lift the cooled plums from the butter sauce and transfer them to the prepared plate, cut sides down. In a small bowl, whisk the egg yolk until it is smooth. Scoop 1 teaspoon of the egg yolk into a medium bowl along with the cream cheese, confectioners' sugar, and vanilla extract. Whisk until well combined and smooth. To the small bowl with the remaining egg yolk, add 1 teaspoon of water and whisk to combine. Set the plums, cream cheese filling, and egg wash aside.

Remove the Rough Puff Pastry Dough from the refrigerator and cut the dough in half crosswise. Cover one half of the dough with plastic wrap and return to the refrigerator. Lightly dust a clean work surface with flour and roll the remaining dough into a 10-inch / 25cm square. Cut the rolled dough into four 5-inch / 13cm squares. Transfer three of the dough squares onto one of the prepared baking sheets and refrigerate.

Fold the remaining dough square in half diagonally to form a triangle. With the longest side facing toward you (the side of the triangle that is folded over), use a sharp knife to make two cuts ½ inch from the outside edges of the triangles but do not cut through the tip of the triangle. There should be a ½-inch gap at the top between the two cuts. Open the triangle and lightly brush the outer edges of the dough square with the egg wash. Gently lift the right-hand strip of the pastry over to the left and lightly press it onto the inner square of the pastry. Gently lift the left-hand strip of the pastry over to the right and lightly press it onto the inner square of the pastry. The pastry should look similar to a square picture frame. Use a fork to prick the bottom of the inner pastry three times, then top with one-eighth of the cream cheese filling (about 1 tablespoon) and a roasted plum half, cut side down. The cream cheese filling and plum should fit snugly within the "frame" of the pastry. Bring the baking sheet with the chilled dough squares out of the refrigerator and use a large metal spatula to transfer the formed Danish to it, then place the baking sheet back in the fridge to keep cool. Repeat to make 7 additional Danishes, transferring the Danishes to the baking sheets as they are formed (4 Danishes per baking sheet). Chill the formed Danishes for 1 hour.

About 15 minutes before the 1-hour mark, preheat the oven to 400°F / 200°C.

Lightly brush the edges of the dough on 4 of the Danishes with some of the remaining egg wash and bake until puffed and deep golden brown, about 30 minutes, rotating the baking sheet once after 20 minutes. Transfer the Danishes to a cooling rack and cool completely. Repeat to bake and cool the second batch of Danishes. Dust the cooled Danishes lightly with confectioners' sugar and serve.

Spiced Puff Pastry Pull-Apart Muffins with Cherry Jam

PREP TIME: 20 minutes
COOK TIME: 30 minutes

⅓ cup / 65g granulated sugar

1¼ teaspoons ground cinnamon

¼ teaspoon ground cardamom

¼ teaspoon ground ginger

¼ teaspoon kosher salt

1 sheet Rough Puff Pastry Dough, chilled (page 160)

All-purpose flour, for dusting

2 tablespoons unsalted butter, at room temperature

1 egg

¼ cup / 80g cherry jam

Lightly spray a 12-cup nonstick muffin pan with nonstick cooking spray and set aside.

In a small bowl, combine the sugar, cinnamon, cardamom, ginger, and salt. Stir to combine, then set aside.

Cut the Rough Puff Pastry Dough in half crosswise. Cover one half of the dough with plastic wrap and return it to the refrigerator. Lightly dust a clean work surface with flour and roll the remaining dough into a 10-inch / 25cm square. Spread 1 tablespoon of the butter evenly onto the dough, then sprinkle with half of the spiced sugar. Lightly press the spiced sugar into the butter and the dough. Cut the dough lengthwise into three equal pieces. With the longer side of the dough facing you, roll each piece of dough into a swirled log then cut each log crosswise into eight equal pieces (twenty-four pieces total). Arrange four pieces, cut sides up, in each of six of the prepared muffin cups. Repeat with the remaining dough, butter, and spiced sugar to make 12 muffins total. Refrigerate the muffins for 20 minutes while you preheat the oven.

Preheat the oven to 400°F / 200°C.

In a small bowl, whisk together the egg and a splash of water. Brush the top of the chilled muffins with the egg wash and set the muffin pan on a baking sheet. Bake until the dough is puffed and deep golden brown, 25 to 30 minutes, rotating the baking sheet once after 15 minutes.

Cool the muffins in the pan for 10 minutes, then transfer to a room-temperature baking sheet to cool completely. Once the muffins are cooled, use the fat end of a chopstick to create a small hole in the center of each muffin, but be careful to not go all the way to the bottom. Spoon the cherry jam into a small piping bag. Pipe some of the cherry jam into the center of each muffin and serve immediately.

Salt-and-Pepper Cheese Twists
with Honey Drizzle

PREP TIME: 20 minutes
COOK TIME: 25 minutes

———

¼ cup / 15g grated pecorino cheese

1 sheet Rough Puff Pastry Dough (page 160), chilled

1½ ounces / 40g finely shredded aged sharp Cheddar cheese (about ¾ cup)

1 teaspoon flaky sea salt

Coarsely ground black pepper

1 tablespoon honey, plus more for serving

Line two baking sheets with parchment and set aside.

Sprinkle the pecorino cheese onto a clean work surface and spread the cheese out into a 10 by 16-inch / 25 by 40cm rectangle. Top with the Rough Puff Pastry Dough and lightly roll out the dough into a rectangle that is the same dimensions as the cheese. As you roll out the dough, make sure that the pecorino cheese is getting pressed into the underside of the dough.

Sprinkle the top of the dough with the shredded Cheddar cheese, then top with the flaky sea salt and several large grinds of black pepper. Using the rolling pin and rolling in an upward motion, press the cheese and seasoning into the dough. Cut the dough crosswise into sixteen equal strips about 1 inch / 2.5cm thick (they do not have to be perfect). Transfer the dough strips to the prepared baking sheets, eight per baking sheet, spacing the strips evenly apart. Twist each strip several times to create a spiraled effect, using your fingers to lightly press the ends of the dough onto the parchment paper (this will help the twists keep their shape). Refrigerate the cheese twists for 20 minutes while you preheat the oven.

Position two racks in the upper-middle and lower-middle center of the oven and preheat to 400°F / 200°C.

Bake until the twists are puffed and deep golden brown, 20 to 25 minutes, rotating the baking sheets top to bottom and front to back once after 15 minutes.

Cool on the baking sheets for just 5 minutes—do not let them sit too long, or the cheese will stick completely to the parchment paper. Transfer to a serving platter and drizzle with the honey. Serve with additional honey on the side.

Widogast's Nein-Layered Tower (of Pancakes)

Want to impress your friends with some food wizardry, but are intimidated by complex gastronomical techniques? Try some dunamancy instead, and make gravity work for you! This tower of sweetness recalls Caleb's magnificent magical edifice, but without the hours of toil he spent researching and assembling it. This is just slather, stack, and repeat, all the way to the top. Feel free to customize your tower to your audience's desires—jam, thinly sliced fruit, or mini chocolate chips would all go well between the layers—but embellish with a light touch, lest the weight increase too much and the dunamantic weaving tip out of control.* Top with cream cheese glaze—we've dyed ours to evoke the Luxon beacon—and garnish with the treats of your choice.

Sorry, got carried away there: don't put too much stuff on the pile or it'll collapse.

PREP TIME: 30 minutes
**COOK TIME: 1 hour
30 minutes**

────

Pancakes

3½ cups / 490g all-purpose flour

¼ cup / 50g granulated sugar

¼ cup / 50g packed dark brown sugar

2¼ teaspoons baking powder

2¼ teaspoons baking soda

1½ teaspoons kosher salt

3½ cups / 830ml buttermilk, at room temperature, plus more if needed

3 eggs, at room temperature

*T*O MAKE THE PANCAKES: In a large bowl, whisk together the flour, granulated sugar, brown sugar, baking powder, baking soda, and salt. In a medium bowl, combine the buttermilk, eggs, and vanilla extract and whisk until smooth. Whisk in the melted butter. Pour the egg mixture into the flour mixture and whisk until combined, being careful not to overmix (some small lumps are okay). The batter will be very thick and similar to cake batter, which will make for sturdy yet tender-crumbed pancakes that will hold up well as they are stacked. Let the batter rest for 15 minutes. After resting, the batter should still be thick but drizzle off of a rubber spatula or spoon in very thick ribbons. Stir in a splash or two of additional buttermilk, if needed, to ensure the batter is this consistency. Line a large baking sheet with parchment paper and set aside.

When the batter is ready, heat a 10-inch / 25cm nonstick skillet over medium heat. Lightly brush with some canola oil. Scoop or pour a scant ¾ cup / 175ml of the batter into the center of the skillet and spread the batter out to form an 8-inch / 20cm pancake. Cook until large bubbles begin to burst all over the surface of the batter, the edges of the pancake are starting to become dry, and the bottom is golden brown, 4 to 7 minutes.

1 tablespoon vanilla
extract

6 tablespoons / 85g
unsalted butter, melted
and cooled slightly

Canola oil, for greasing
the skillet (about
1½ tablespoons)

Cream Cheese Frosting and Glaze

Three 8-ounce / 225g
packages cream cheese, at
room temperature

4 cups / 480g
confectioners' sugar

6 to 8 tablespoons / 90 to
120ml milk

4 teaspoons vanilla extract

Violet concentrated food
coloring or gel, as needed

Black concentrated food
coloring or gel, as needed

1 cup (2 sticks) / 220g
unsalted butter, at room
temperature

Finely grated zest from
2 large lemons (about
1 tablespoon, lightly
packed)

Carefully flip the pancake and cook until the bottom is golden brown, about 3 more minutes. Transfer to the prepared baking sheet. Repeat with the remaining batter to make 8 more pancakes, brushing the skillet with additional oil as needed. Layer the pancakes in two stacks as you cook them. Let the pancakes cool completely.

TO MAKE THE CREAM CHEESE FROSTING AND GLAZE: In a medium bowl, combine one 8-ounce / 225g package of cream cheese and 1 cup / 120g of the confectioners' sugar. Use a rubber spatula to stir the sugar into the cream cheese until mostly combined. Switch to an electric handheld mixer and beat on medium-high until smooth and well combined. Add 4 tablespoons / 60ml of the milk and 2 teaspoons of the vanilla extract and beat until smooth. Beat in additional milk, 1 tablespoon at a time, until the mixture easily drizzles off of a spoon. The consistency of the glaze should be similar to creamy tahini or really thick maple syrup. Pour half of the glaze into a small bowl. Stir violet concentrated food coloring or gel into each bowl of white glaze to make one a dark violet color and one a lighter lavender color. To darken the violet glaze, stir in black concentrated food coloring or gel, one drop at a time, until the violet color becomes an even darker indigo hue. To make drizzling the glazes easier, you can transfer them into two separate liquid measuring cups with spouts. Set both glazes aside.

recipe continues ☞

Mead Gastrique

½ cup / 120ml dry honey mead

½ cup / 120ml white wine vinegar

¼ cup / 60ml granulated sugar

1 to 2 tablespoons water (optional), plus more as needed

8 to 10 fresh mint leaves, torn

6 to 8 ounces / 170 to 225g Burrata, roughly torn into medium chunks

1 tablespoon Marash chile flakes

1 to 2 tablespoons dry honey mead

Top the salad with the chunks of Burrata, remaining 1½ tablespoons olive oil, and Marash chile flakes. Drizzle the 1 to 2 tablespoons of mead over the salad and season with salt and pepper.

NOTE: If Cara Caras and pomelos are not available in your area, substitute regular navel oranges and pink grapefruit.

Yasha's Bug Bites

The warriors of Xhorhas's Iothia Moorland are accomplished hunters of all types of game, be it big or small. During Yasha's time with the Dolorav clan, she acquired a taste for the smallest creatures: rodents, spiders, and insects. One of her favorite treats is crunchy bugs, such as these crickets. Now, both we and Yasha understand that not everyone is delighted by the idea of eating bugs. You can do this with chickpeas instead; they just take longer to dry. One other note: The spice mix isn't true to Moorland-style roasted crickets; rather, it's inspired by the way Yasha's bugs were served during Jester's elaborate magical feasts, an old childhood favorite given new life.

PREP TIME: 15 minutes
COOK TIME: 12 minutes

———

2 tablespoons dark brown sugar

1 tablespoon garlic powder

1 tablespoon instant coffee

1 tablespoon black lemon pepper

½ tablespoon powdered mustard

½ tablespoon smoked paprika

½ tablespoon celery salt

One 1-ounce / 30g bag freeze-dried house crickets (for human consumption), plain, *or*
one 15-ounce / 425g can chickpeas in water (see Note for preparation)

2 tablespoons olive oil

Kosher salt

Preheat the oven to 400°F / 200°C and line a baking sheet with parchment paper.

In a small bowl, thoroughly combine the brown sugar, garlic powder, instant coffee, black lemon pepper, powdered mustard, smoked paprika, and celery salt. Set aside.

In a medium bowl, toss the crickets with the olive oil. Sprinkle in the seasoning mixture, 1 tablespoon at a time, and toss well, until the crickets are fully coated. Season with kosher salt.

Spread the crickets on the prepared baking sheet. Bake for 10 to 12 minutes, until crispy and fragrant. While roasting, toss once at the 5-minute mark and rotate the pan. Line a bowl with a paper towel. As soon as the crickets are done, transfer to the lined bowl and serve immediately.

NOTE: If using chickpeas, be sure to drain well and pat them down with a towel to remove excess moisture, 4 to 6 hours before preparing. Spread the chickpeas out on a baking sheet lined with parchment paper and set aside to dry. Follow the instructions as you would for the crickets, but roast the chickpeas for 25 minutes, or until crunchy. While roasting, toss once at the 15-minute mark and rotate the pan.

Brenattos' Unexpected Guests

When the Mighty Nein were at the height of their adventuring, they would often need to be someplace fast. With Caleb's powerful magic, the time between realizing they needed to be someplace and arriving there was reduced to seconds. This was often a shock to the people at their destination, whom they had forgotten to warn before teleporting in. Once, they arrived hungry in the Brenattos' living room in Nicodranas and found only some hummus and carrots in the pantry. But the Brenattos are no humdrum family, and Yeza's hummus is no plain hummus. The added beet provides a gorgeous color, another layer of flavor, and a way to sneak an extra variety of vegetable into a kid who is sometimes, maybe, a little averse.

PREP TIME: 15 minutes
COOK TIME: 1 hour

¼ cup / 60ml water

¼ cup / 60ml red wine vinegar, plus more to taste

¼ cup / 60ml extra-virgin olive oil, plus more for drizzling

4 garlic cloves, lightly smashed

Kosher salt and freshly ground black pepper

12 ounces / 340g red beets, peeled and cut into ¾-inch chunks

One 15.5-ounce / 439g can chickpeas, drained and rinsed well

⅓ cup / 95g tahini

¾ teaspoon toasted sesame seeds

Peeled baby rainbow carrots, for serving

Preheat the oven to 375°F / 190°C. In an 8-inch / 20cm glass or ceramic baking dish, stir together 3 tablespoons of the water, 3 tablespoons of the vinegar, 2 tablespoons of the olive oil, the garlic, and a large pinch of salt and pepper. Add the beets and gently stir to coat in the cooking liquid. Cover the baking dish with aluminum foil and bake until the beets are fork-tender, about 1 hour, stirring the beets once after 30 minutes.

Remove from the oven, take off the foil, stir in the chickpeas, and cool the beets and chickpeas on a rack for 20 minutes. Transfer the dish contents along with any remaining liquid to a food processor. Add the tahini and the remaining 1 tablespoon water, 1 tablespoon vinegar, and 2 tablespoons olive oil. Season with salt and pepper and blend until very smooth and creamy, scraping down the sides of the bowl as needed. If the mixture is really thick, blend in a splash or two of additional water. Season with additional salt, pepper, and red wine vinegar if needed.

Spoon the hummus into a shallow serving bowl, drizzle with additional olive oil, and sprinkle with the toasted sesame seeds. Serve with peeled baby rainbow carrots for dipping.

NOTE: Transfer any leftover hummus to an airtight container and store in the refrigerator for up to 5 days.

The Frost Worm Stew of Den Thelyss

Some aspects of the Kryn Dynasty practice of consecration are, by necessity, closely guarded secrets. But we do know that when a new person is welcomed into one of the Dens, either by birth or adoption, a celebration is in order. In Den Thelyss, the family of Essek Thelyss and one of the three ruling Dens in the Dynasty, the celebration includes an elaborate feast. A staple of the feast is this hearty stew of root vegetables, herbed dumplings, and the rarest meat the Den's hunters can procure. Frost worm is a special favorite, but considering that frost worm meat must be procured from the Biting North at great peril and expense, we've substituted venison or beef here.*

Please do not travel to the Biting North in search of frost worm meat. Venison is pretty close, especially after cooking. We swear.

PREP TIME: 45 minutes
COOK TIME: 2 to 3 hours

---

2 pounds / 900g venison chuck steak or beef, sinews removed and cubed into large 2-inch / 5cm chunks

2 tablespoons all-purpose flour

Kosher salt and freshly ground black pepper

2 tablespoons olive oil

1 large yellow onion, small diced

2 large carrots, medium diced

2 cups / 475ml water

3 cups / 710ml beef broth

½ cup / 120ml Chinese cooking wine

3 Japanese mild curry cubes

Heat a large heavy-bottomed pot over medium-high heat. While it is heating, in a small bowl, toss the venison with the flour and season with salt and pepper. Set aside.

Lower the heat to medium and add the olive oil, onion, and carrots. Season with salt and pepper and stir until the veggies are soft, 3 to 4 minutes.

Push the veggies to one side of the pot and add the venison. Allow to brown on all sides, flipping pieces so that they brown evenly, 3 to 5 minutes.

Once the venison is browned, add the water, 1½ cups / 360ml of the beef broth, the Chinese cooking wine, and the Japanese curry cubes, and stir. Cover, lower the heat, and simmer until the meat is almost tender and the curry cubes are dissolved, 2 to 3 hours. Check the stew occasionally to give it a stir and make sure the liquid level is adequate. If it's too low, add a bit of water or beef broth and slightly lower the heat.

1 large yucca, peeled and large diced (or any waxy potato)

1 large Braeburn, Honeycrisp, or Jonagold apple, peeled, cored, and large diced

Herbed Dumpling Dough

1½ cups / 210g all-purpose flour

1 teaspoon baking powder

1 teaspoon kosher salt

½ cup / 120ml buttermilk

2 tablespoons fresh thyme leaves, finely minced

1 tablespoon finely minced fresh sage leaves

1 tablespoon finely minched fresh chives

1 tablespoon unsalted butter, at room temperature

1 bunch chives, finely chopped, for garnish

WHILE THE STEW IS SIMMERING, MAKE THE HERBED DUMPLING DOUGH: Lightly grease a sheet of parchment paper with nonstick cooking spray. Sift the flour, baking powder, and salt into a medium bowl. Add the buttermilk, thyme, sage, minced chives, and butter and mix together until a dough forms and the herbs are well incorporated.

Roll out sixteen 1-inch / 2.5cm balls and set on the greased parchment paper until ready to cook.

Forty-five minutes before the stew is done, when the beef is almost fork-tender, stir in the yucca and add the remaining 1½ cups of beef broth. Season with salt and pepper and cover.

When the yucca is still firm but able to be pierced with a fork, after 20 to 30 minutes, stir in the apple. Drop the dumpling dough balls where there is at least ¼ inch of stew liquid and cook uncovered for 10 minutes. Flip the dumplings, cover, and cook for an additional 10 minutes. The dumplings are done when the dough is billowy and cooked in the center.

Before serving, season with salt and pepper. Place a generous helping of stew in each bowl and top with 3 or 4 dumplings. Garnish with chopped chives.

Shadowshire Soup

Underneath the city of Rosohna lies a huge subterranean cavern lined with crops, many of them growing only with the aid of magic. Some resemble more conventional root vegetables, in taste at least, while others offer an experience all their own. We cannot assume you have access to Shadowshire produce, so we have attempted to re-create the flavor of one of their popular soups using a blend of ingredients that are easier to find outside of Rosohna. Purists, of course, will argue that Shadowshire Soup is nothing without freshly grated yuyo. They will further note our soup's total inability to glow in the dark. We humbly submit that we have done our best.

PREP TIME: 25 minutes
COOK TIME: 1 hour 20 minutes

---

4 tablespoons / 55g unsalted butter

3 cups / 420g diced yellow onions (from about 2 large onions)

1½ cups / 165g diced celery (from about 3 stalks)

3 tablespoons tomato paste

5 garlic cloves, minced

2 teaspoons chopped fresh thyme leaves (from about 10 sprigs)

Kosher salt and freshly ground black pepper

1 teaspoon paprika, preferably smoked (see Note)

½ teaspoon caraway seeds

In a large heavy-bottomed pot or Dutch oven over medium heat, melt the butter. Add the onions and celery and cook, stirring often, until soft and translucent, 5 to 7 minutes. Add the tomato paste, garlic, thyme, 1 teaspoon of salt, ½ teaspoon of black pepper, the paprika, and caraway seeds and stir to evenly coat the vegetables in the tomato paste. Cook, stirring often, until the tomato paste darkens slightly and starts to stick to the bottom of the pot, 4 to 7 minutes.

Add the vegetable stock and canned diced tomatoes with their juices and scrape the bottom of the pot to release any brown bits stuck to the bottom. Add the potatoes, beets, carrots, and bay leaves. Bring the mixture to a simmer and cook until the potatoes and beets are tender enough to easily pierce with a knife, 50 to 60 minutes. Stir in the cabbage and cook just until the cabbage is tender and wilted, 5 to 8 minutes.

recipe and ingredients continue ☞

7 cups / 1.7L unsalted vegetable stock

One 14.5-ounce / 411g can diced tomatoes

1 pound / 450g Yukon Gold potatoes (about 4 large), peeled and cut into ½-inch pieces

1½ pounds / 680g red beets (about 4 medium), peeled and cut into 1-inch / 2.5 cm pieces

2 large carrots, peeled and sliced into ¼-inch-thick rounds (about 1¾ cups / 210g)

2 dried bay leaves

2 cups / 100g finely shredded green cabbage (from about one-third of a medium head of cabbage)

2 tablespoons lemon juice (from about 1 medium lemon)

Sour cream, chopped chives, and dill, for topping (optional)

Remove the soup from the heat. Remove and discard the bay leaves and stir in the lemon juice. Season with salt and pepper. Serve the soup with a dollop of sour cream, chives, and dill, if desired.

NOTE: Smoked paprika can be found in the spice section of most well-stocked grocery stores, often labeled pimenton or Spanish paprika. If unavailable, regular paprika can be used instead.

Asarius's Prized Meat Pies

Every year, droves of Xhorhasians make their way west to Asarius, the City of Beasts, for the city's Faire of Abundance. There, Asarians, traders, and cooks from across the land show off their proudest culinary creations in a food festival that lasts for two days. Food is bought, sold, and thoroughly enjoyed, but running underneath the merriment is a fierce competition. On the second day, the ten most promising creations are sampled by members of Den Olios. The winner is awarded a sizable coin purse along with the Golden Thistle, a trophy presented by Lady Olios herself. We are proud to present to you the Golden Thistle recipe from 842 PD, a delectable meat pie created by an anonymous local baker who took the purse and skipped town. He only stopped long enough to sell the recipe twice, to us and to the Four Corners Tavern, which now serves pie on fight nights.

PREP TIME: 25 minutes
COOK TIME: 40 minutes

Dough

⅓ cup / 80ml lukewarm water

One ¼-ounce / 7g packet active dry yeast (2½ teaspoons)

1 tablespoon granulated sugar

6 tablespoons / 90g unsalted butter

¾ cup / 175ml whole milk

4 cups / 560g all-purpose flour, plus more for dusting

1 teaspoon kosher salt

2 large eggs

1 tablespoon water

*T*O MAKE THE DOUGH: In a small bowl, combine the water, yeast, and sugar. Stir to dissolve the sugar and let sit at room temperature until foamy, 10 to 15 minutes.

While the yeast is activating, in a small pot over medium heat, melt the butter, stirring often, just until melted but not sizzling, 2 to 3 minutes. Remove the pot from the heat and add the milk.

Add both the yeast and milk mixtures to the bowl of a stand mixer fitted with a dough hook. Add the flour and salt and mix on medium-low speed until the dough sticks to the hook in one mass and no pockets of unincorporated flour remain, 2 to 3 minutes. (If kneading the dough by hand, mix with a rubber spatula until almost all of the flour has been absorbed into the dough, then turn out the dough onto a lightly floured surface and knead by hand until smooth, 5 to 7 minutes.)

Remove the dough from the mixing bowl, coat the inside of the bowl with nonstick cooking spray, and transfer the dough back to the bowl. Tightly wrap the bowl in plastic wrap and let rise at room temperature until puffy and almost doubled in size, 1 to 1½ hours.

recipe and ingredients continue ↪

Meat Filling

3 tablespoons olive oil

¾ pound / 340g Yukon Gold potatoes, peeled and cut into ¼-inch cubes (about 3 large potatoes)

1 large yellow onion, diced (about 1½ cups / 210g)

1 large carrot, peeled and diced (about 1 cup / 140g)

2 large celery ribs, diced (about 1 cup / 110g)

1 pound / 450g lean ground beef

3 garlic cloves, minced

2 teaspoons chopped fresh thyme leaves (from about 10 sprigs)

1½ teaspoons kosher salt

1 teaspoon freshly ground black pepper

NOTE: The assembled, unbaked pies can be frozen in an individual layer on a tightly wrapped baking sheet for several months. When ready to bake, let sit uncovered at room temperature for 2 hours before baking, then proceed with the baking instructions.

WHILE THE DOUGH IS RISING, MAKE THE MEAT FILLING: In a large high-sided pan or Dutch oven over medium heat, heat the olive oil. Add the potatoes and cook, stirring occasionally, until just starting to soften, 5 to 7 minutes. Add the onion, carrot, and celery and cook, stirring often, until the onion is light golden brown and the carrot is softened, 8 to 11 minutes. Add the ground beef and immediately break it up into small pieces with the back of a spatula. Cook, stirring often, until the beef is cooked through and no red remains, 3 to 5 minutes. Add the garlic, thyme, salt, and pepper and cook, stirring constantly, until fragrant, 3 to 5 minutes. Remove the filling from the heat and let cool for at least 30 minutes before assembling the hand pies.

TO ASSEMBLE THE PIES: Set two oven racks at the upper-middle and lower-middle positions and preheat the oven to 350°F / 175°C. Lightly flour a work surface. Line two baking sheets with parchment paper or nonstick baking mats. Crack the eggs into a small bowl and add the water. Mix with a fork until no streaks of egg yolks remain.

Punch the dough down to deflate it and transfer to the floured surface. Divide the dough into ten equal pieces (about 3 ounces / 85g per piece) and roll into balls. Using a rolling pin, roll each ball into a 5-inch / 13cm circle that's ¼ inch thick. Place ⅓ cup / 70g of the filling in the center of each circle. Brush the outside edge of each circle with the beaten eggs. Fold one side of the dough over the filling and press it onto the other side of the dough to create a half-moon shape. (You will need to stretch the dough slightly.) Crimp the edges of the pies with the tines of a fork. Carefully transfer them to the prepared baking sheets, 5 pies per sheet. Use a sharp knife to make three horizontal cuts in the top of each pie. Brush the pies with the eggs and bake, rotating the pans from top to bottom halfway through baking, until light golden brown, 20 to 25 minutes. Let cool on the baking sheets for at least 10 minutes before serving.

Caduceus's Ethically Sourced Mushroom Toasts

Caduceus Clay, as a dedicated servant of the Wildmother, also serves the natural cycle of life and death. He gladly heals the sick and the injured when possible, and he returns the dead to the earth with equal aplomb. His decomposition spells cause the remains to sprout plants and fungi, so Caduceus gathers these byproducts and cooks with them. Are we saying that we sampled sandwiches made, at one step removed, from corpses? Yes.* Are we saying that you need to make your sandwich the same way? No. But if you do, make sure to thank the person whose grave you're harvesting. Never hurts to be polite.

But, as Caduceus pointed out, aren't most things one step removed from corpses, really?

PREP TIME: 10 minutes
COOK TIME: 25 minutes

———

5 tablespoons / 70g unsalted butter

Four ¾-inch-thick slices of sourdough or country bread

1½ pounds / 680g cremini or white button mushrooms, trimmed and quartered

4 garlic cloves, minced

1 teaspoon chopped fresh rosemary leaves (from about 1 medium sprig)

1 teaspoon chopped fresh thyme leaves (from about 5 sprigs)

Kosher salt and freshly ground black pepper

1 cup / 240g whole milk ricotta cheese

½ cup / 10g arugula

Extra-virgin olive oil, for drizzling

In a large cast-iron or nonstick skillet over medium heat, melt 1 tablespoon of the butter. Add two slices of the bread and toast, flipping once, until golden brown on both sides, 1½ to 2 minutes per side. Transfer the toasts to serving plates and add 1 tablespoon of butter to the pan. Once the butter is melted, add the remaining two slices of bread and repeat the cooking process, transferring them to serving plates when toasted.

Add the remaining 3 tablespoons of butter to the pan and swirl to evenly coat it. Add the mushrooms and cook, stirring often, until they have released their moisture and shrunk in size and are just starting to brown, 9 to 11 minutes.

Add the garlic, rosemary, thyme, ¾ teaspoon salt, and ½ teaspoon pepper and stir to evenly coat the mushrooms. Continue cooking over medium heat, stirring often, until the mushrooms are deep golden brown, 4 to 6 minutes more. Remove the pan from the heat and set aside.

Spread each slice of toast with ¼ cup / 60g ricotta cheese and top with one-fourth of the cooked mushrooms. Divide the arugula over the tops and drizzle with olive oil. Season with additional salt and pepper to taste and serve immediately.

Fish Tacos, a Romantic Creation by Guest Chef Frumpkin

When we heard that Beau and Yasha's romance began in earnest with an elaborate magical date featuring tacos, we put out word that we would love the recipe. Imagine our surprise when a cat walked into our test kitchen and jumped up on the counter. There was a note in his mouth bearing only the name of this dish and the word "Achten!" As soon as we looked up from the note, the cat began to assemble the tacos, knocking ingredients off of pantry shelves, batting seasonings across the floor, nudging us toward the stove, hunting bugs to use for garnish,* rolling his eyes at how slow we were to catch on. A steep learning curve, a very messy kitchen, and several chin scritches later, we had these tasty tacos.

*We have substituted black sesame seeds, as the bug-hunting process will be cumbersome for most home cooks.

PREP TIME: 20 minutes
COOK TIME: 15 minutes

———

¼ cup / 60ml olive oil

¼ cup / 60ml fresh lime juice (from about 2 medium limes)

1 teaspoon chili powder

½ teaspoon ground cumin

1½ teaspoons kosher salt

1½ pounds / 680g cod, mahi-mahi, or other flaky whitefish

1 tablespoon sesame oil

1 tablespoon honey, agave, or maple syrup

1 garlic clove, minced

3 cups / 150g thinly sliced red or green cabbage (from about half a medium head of cabbage)

In a large bowl, combine 2 tablespoons of the olive oil, 2 tablespoons of the lime juice, the chili powder, cumin, and 1 teaspoon of the salt. Cut the fish into eight 3-inch / 7.5cm pieces, add to the bowl, and toss to evenly coat them. Let marinate at room temperature for 20 minutes.

While the fish is marinating, in a large bowl, combine the remaining 2 tablespoons of lime juice and ½ teaspoon of salt with the sesame oil, honey, and garlic. Add the cabbage, cilantro, red onion, green onion, jalapeño, and sesame seeds. Toss to evenly coat the vegetables in the dressing and set aside.

Remove the fish from the marinade and pat dry with paper towels, discarding the marinade. In a large nonstick or cast-iron skillet over medium heat, heat the remaining 2 tablespoons of olive oil. Cook the fish in a single layer until the bottoms start to brown, 3 to 4 minutes. Flip and continue cooking the fish until the flesh is completely opaque, 2 to 3 minutes more. Transfer the cooked fish to a large plate and tent with foil to keep warm.

½ cup / 20g coarsely chopped fresh cilantro leaves, plus more for garnish (optional)

Half a small red onion, thinly sliced (about ⅔ cup / 80g)

3 green onions, white and green parts, thinly sliced (about ½ cup / 40g)

1 medium jalapeño, thinly sliced (about ½ cup / 40g)

1 tablespoon black sesame seeds

Eight 4-inch / 10cm corn tortillas

Lime wedges, sliced avocado, and sour cream, for serving (optional)

Wipe out the bottom of the skillet with a paper towel and return it to medium heat. Place 2 or 3 tortillas in the bottom of the pan in a single layer and cook until the tortillas are warm and just starting to char on the bottom, about 60 seconds. Transfer the tortillas to a plate and repeat with the remaining tortillas.

To assemble the tacos, top each tortilla with a piece of fish and about ⅓ cup / 45g of the slaw. Serve with lime wedges, sliced avocado, sour cream, and additional cilantro on top, if desired.

Yasha's flower Cake

To honor her fallen wife Zuala, Yasha Nydoorin gathered flowers from across Exandria and brought them to her grave. After settling down with Beau, Yasha started a new flower collection; their garden used seeds from the Blooming Grove and expanded whenever a new blossom caught her eye. Inspired by Caduceus, Yasha experimented with these flowers by using them in various foods. Many of the early experiments were unsuccessful. Some were hilarious. A few were even edible. Eventually she perfected this cake, flavored with lavender and topped with whatever beautiful flowers* are in season.

*Just make sure they're digestible by humans.**

**That was one of the less hilarious experiments.

PREP TIME: 20 minutes
COOK TIME: 1 hour

Lavender Lemon Cake

½ cup (1 stick) / 110g unsalted butter

2 tablespoons dried lavender, lightly crushed with your fingers (see Note)

2 cups / 280g all-purpose flour

1 tablespoon baking powder

½ teaspoon kosher salt

1 cup / 200g granulated sugar

2 tablespoons lemon zest (from about 2 large lemons)

3 large eggs

TO MAKE THE LAVENDER LEMON CAKE: In a medium saucepan over medium heat, melt the butter. Remove from the heat, stir in the dried lavender, and let cool at room temperature for 20 minutes, stirring occasionally.

Preheat the oven to 350°F / 175°C. Coat a 9-inch / 23cm round cake pan with cooking spray and line the bottom with parchment paper. In a large bowl, whisk together the flour, baking powder, and salt. Set aside.

In a large bowl, combine the granulated sugar and lemon zest. Massage the zest into the sugar with your hands until the sugar is tinged a light golden yellow and is very fragrant.

Strain the melted lavender butter through a fine-mesh strainer into the bowl of lemon sugar, pressing down on the lavender with a spatula to squeeze out the butter, and discard the lavender. Add the eggs, yogurt, and vanilla extract and whisk until smooth. Add the dry ingredients and stir with a rubber spatula just until the batter comes together and no pockets of dry flour remain. Scrape the batter into the cake pan and smooth it out into an even layer. Bake for 45 to 55 minutes, until the top is dark golden brown and a toothpick inserted into the center comes out clean with just

recipe and ingredients continue ☞

1⅓ cups / 320g plain full-fat yogurt (not Greek)

1 tablespoon vanilla extract

Vanilla Frosting

One 8-ounce / 225g block full-fat cream cheese, at room temperature

4 tablespoons / 55g unsalted butter, at room temperature

2 cups / 240g confectioners' sugar

1 teaspoon vanilla extract

¼ teaspoon kosher salt

Edible flowers such as marigolds, pansies, and lavender, for garnish (optional)

a few moist crumbs attached. Remove from the oven and let cool in the pan for 10 minutes, then carefully invert it onto a cooling rack and let cool for at least 1 hour.

TO MAKE THE VANILLA FROSTING: In the bowl of a stand mixer fitted with the paddle attachment, combine the cream cheese, butter, confectioners' sugar, vanilla, and salt. (Alternatively, use a large mixing bowl and electric handheld mixer.) Slowly increase the mixer speed to medium-high and whip until smooth and fluffy, 1½ to 2½ minutes. Makes about 1⅔ cups.

To assemble the cake, transfer it to a large serving plate or cake stand. Add the frosting to the top of the cake and smooth into an even layer using an offset spatula or the back of a spoon. Garnish with edible flowers, if using.

NOTE: Dried lavender can be found in the spice or tea sections of specialty grocery stores or easily ordered online. Just make sure the lavender you're purchasing is meant for culinary use and is labeled food-grade.

Black Moss Cupcakes

Have you always wanted to visit Uthodurn, but the thought of travel through the Flotket Alps leaves you cold? Now you can have a taste of this famed Dwarven/Elven city without leaving your home. The Softer Stoneforge bakery's original recipe calls for actual black moss, so we've substituted easier-to-find ingredients that still put an earthy spin on the traditional sweet cupcake. And for an extra-*charming* treat, try a sprinkle of our Dust of Deliciousness.*

Exquisite Exandria disavows responsibility for any actions, pacts, transformations, transmutations, friendships, courtships, understandings, or misunderstandings resulting from the use of Dust of Deliciousness.

PREP TIME: 30 minutes
COOK TIME: 20 minutes

___

Dark Chocolate Cupcakes

1 cup / 140g all-purpose flour

¾ cup / 150g granulated sugar

⅓ cup / 25g unsweetened natural cocoa powder

¾ teaspoon baking soda

½ teaspoon baking powder

½ teaspoon kosher salt

1 large egg

⅔ cup / 80ml whole milk

⅓ cup / 80g sour cream

2 tablespoons vegetable oil

2 teaspoons vanilla extract

2 or 3 drops black food coloring (optional)

To MAKE THE DARK CHOCOLATE CUPCAKES: Set a rack in the middle of the oven and preheat to 325°F / 165°C. Line the cups of a 12-cup standard muffin tin with paper cupcake liners.

In a large bowl, whisk together the flour, sugar, cocoa powder, baking soda, baking powder, and salt. In a second large mixing bowl, whisk together the egg, milk, sour cream, vegetable oil, vanilla extract, and black food coloring (if using) until no streaks of egg yolk remain. Add the dry ingredients to the wet and mix with a rubber spatula just until a smooth batter forms and no pockets of dry flour remain.

Fill each cupcake liner about two-thirds full. Bake, rotating the pan front to back halfway through baking, 16 to 19 minutes, until a toothpick inserted into the center of a cupcake comes out with just a few moist crumbs attached. Let cool slightly, then transfer the cupcakes onto a cooling rack and let cool completely.

To MAKE THE CHOCOLATE-MATCHA FROSTING: In the bowl of a stand mixer fitted with the paddle attachment, combine the butter, cream cheese, confectioners' sugar, cocoa powder, matcha powder, milk, vanilla, and salt. (Alternatively, use a large mixing bowl and electric handheld mixer.) Mix on low speed just until the ingredients are

recipe and ingredients continue ↪

Chocolate-Matcha Frosting

4 tablespoons / 55g unsalted butter, softened

2 ounces / 55g full-fat cream cheese, at room temperature

1⅓ cups / 160g confectioners' sugar

¼ cup / 20g unsweetened natural cocoa powder

½ teaspoon matcha powder

1 tablespoon whole milk

1 teaspoon vanilla extract

Pinch of kosher salt

Dust of Deliciousness (opposite; optional)

Moss Cookie Crunchies

¾ cup / 40g vanilla wafer cookies such as Nilla Wafers

1½ teaspoons light brown sugar

1½ teaspoons matcha powder

1 tablespoon unsalted butter, melted and cooled slightly

combined, then increase the speed to medium-high and beat until the frosting is light and fluffy, 1½ to 2½ minutes. Transfer the frosting into a large piping bag fitted with a straight tip, or a zip-top bag with one corner snipped off.

TO MAKE THE MOSS COOKIE CRUNCHIES: Place the vanilla wafer cookies in the bowl of a food processor and process until they are the texture of fine sand, 15 to 25 seconds. (Alternatively, place the cookies in a large zip top bag and smash with a rolling pin or skillet.) Transfer the crushed cookies to a large mixing bowl and add the brown sugar and matcha powder. Toss until the cookie crumbs are evenly coated in the matcha powder. Add the melted butter and mix, using your hands, until the crumbs are evenly moistened.

Frost the cupcakes by piping an even, generous layer of frosting on top of each. Working with one cupcake at a time, invert the cupcake and gently press the frosted top into the bowl of cookie crunchies, rotating so the moss sticks to the sides of the frosting, until the top is evenly coated. Repeat this process with the remaining cupcakes. Sprinkle all with Dust of Deliciousness (if using).

Dust of Deliciousness

4 tablespoons █████████
sugar, gathered from
████████████

4 sprigs ███████████,
crushed to powder

6 dried █████████,
crushed to powder (for full
efficacy, ensure that the
██████████ are fully ripe
before picking)

2 teaspoons ████████████,
or more to taste

To make the Dust of Deliciousness: Combine the ████████ and █████████, taking care to never ██.

Slowly add the ███████████ while ████████████████████. Next, flip the ████████████, close your eyes, and ███████████████. Continue █████████████████, peeking occasionally, until the mixture has turned ██████████████. You may now open your eyes fully. Turn away and take a deep breath. Turn back to the mixture, ████████████████████████ ██,

carefully transfer to a small pouch, and seal. Exhale. Wipe down all work surfaces and utensils immediately, and launder all exposed clothing promptly. Let the pouch sit undisturbed for 1 hour, then activate the Dust by ██ ██ ██ ██.*

*On second thought, just use food glitter.

The Ruby of the Sea Cocktail

The Lavish Chateau in Nicodranas is a lovely place to stay: big fancy meals, big fancy drinks, big fancy beds. But what really sets the Chateau apart is their signature performer and courtesan: Marion Lavorre, the Ruby of the Sea. Her charms have delighted guests and clients for decades, but her performances are not long, and her private time is expensive. Many who drop by the Chateau for a meal or a drink therefore leave without getting to see her. Not wishing to resort to something as tacky as merchandise, the Chateau's management arrived at a way to give all guests a small taste, if you will, of the Ruby of the Sea experience. This special cocktail was designed to refresh and relax in equal measure, just like the Ruby herself.

PREP TIME: 4 hours 30 minutes

---

1 cup / 25g dried hibiscus flowers

4 cups / 950ml water, boiling hot

Ice cubes, for serving

4 ounces / 120ml ginger syrup

4 ounces / 120ml mezcal

16 ounces / 475ml tonic water

4 sprigs pineapple mint, for garnish

4 dried lime wheels, for garnish

In a heat-safe pitcher, add the hibiscus flowers and boiling water. Allow the flowers to steep until the water becomes a deep red color and tastes a bit sour, 10 to 20 minutes. Strain, cover, and refrigerate for at least 4 hours.

In four 16-ounce glasses or tumblers, add a few ice cubes and pour 1 ounce / 30ml of ginger syrup into each glass. Next, pour 1 ounce / 30ml of mezcal into each glass and stir with the syrup. Add 1 cup of the hibiscus tea and top with tonic water. Stir again and garnish with a sprig of mint and a lime wheel.

Lionett's Summer Sangria

Beauregard Lionett's family business, the Rainbow Vineyards in Kamordah, is a strange success story. Beau's father, Thoreau, bought a run-down farm on land that was considered difficult to grow on. Thoreau claimed that he understood how to work with the geothermal activity in the area, planting vineyards and various other crops amid the geysers. To everyone's surprise, everything he planted began to thrive, growing and blooming in wild abundance. Lionett makes several types of excellent wines from their grapes; we've used their Sauvignon Blanc, together with rum and a selection of summer fruits, to create this colorful sangria.

PREP TIME: 30 minutes
COOK TIME: 15 minutes

——

1 cup / 128g dried jasmine flowers

1 cup / 240ml water

1 cup / 200g granulated sugar

1 large white peach, pitted and sliced ¼ inch thick

1 medium lemon, cut into ¼-inch-thick wheels

1 medium green apple, cored and medium diced

1 cup / 140g strawberries, hulled and quartered

12 ounces / 360ml dark rum

One 750ml bottle Sauvignon Blanc

Ice cubes, for serving

Mint sprigs, for garnish

In a medium pot, add the jasmine flowers, water, and sugar. Bring to a boil and stir until the sugar is dissolved and the flowers are fragrant, 10 to 12 minutes. Remove from the heat and let cool to room temperature. Once cool, strain the jasmine flowers from the simple syrup.

In a large pitcher, stir together the peach, lemon, apple, strawberries, rum, and Sauvignon Blanc until well incorporated, about 1 minute. Stir in the simple syrup, ¼ cup / 60ml at a time, until the desired sweetness is reached. Stir in enough ice to chill.

To serve, pour into four glasses with additional ice, and garnish with mint sprigs.

The Changebringer's Nectar

In Deastok, Kamordah's sister city to the south, the Grumpy Lily tavern serves two unusual concoctions. While the processes involved in both are extremely labor intensive, we are happy to have developed versions that you can make at home.* This one is a fermented, bubbly creation, unusual enough to bear the name of the goddess of adventure, freedom, and luck. If you've never made your own alcohol before, perhaps plan to stop after the single-fermentation process, so you can properly gauge your creation's strength. If you have the time and temperament for an additional fermentation, the extra effort will add fantastic bubbles to the nectar.**

*For the second recipe, see Schlond's Embrace (page 205).

**Do remember to uncork your nectar for a few seconds between the second and third day of the second fermentation. Otherwise, unless you have the luck of the goddess, the bottles could explode.

PREP TIME: 45 minutes
COOK TIME: 15 minutes
FERMENTATION TIME: 7 to 8 days

½ cup / 50g packed dark brown sugar

6 cups / 1.4L water

1 large pineapple, top and bottom removed

1 cinnamon stick

Sage Simple Syrup

1 cup / 240ml water

1 cup / 200g granulated sugar

20 sprigs sage

Ice cubes, for serving

16 ounces / 475ml sparkling water (optional)

Fresh sage leaves, for garnish

Combine the brown sugar and water in a large pot, and stir until the sugar dissolves.

Rinse the pineapple skin thoroughly in cold water. Slice off the skin, leaving ¼ inch of flesh on the skin, and reserve. Cut the pineapple into wedges, cut off the core, and reserve the core. Store the wedges of pineapple flesh for separate use.

Place the pineapple skin, cinnamon stick, and core in the brown sugar water and stir. To make sure the pineapple skin is fully submerged, place a folded piece of parchment paper on top of the pineapple to weigh it down. Cover the mixture with a tea towel and allow it to ferment at room temperature for 48 to 96 hours.

After 48 hours, check the pineapple mixture for desired fermentation. White froth should be on top of the liquid, and it should smell yeasty, like freshly baked bread. If the mixture has met desired fermentation, strain out the solids and refrigerate for an additional 4 to 8 hours before serving. If the mixture still needs fermentation, cover and allow to ferment for an additional 48 hours.

recipe continues ☞

To make the sage simple syrup: In a medium pot, add the water, granulated sugar, and sage. Bring to a boil then lower to a simmer and stir until the sugar is dissolved and the sage is fragrant, 10 to 12 minutes. Strain to remove the sage leaves, and let cool before using.

To serve, fill a 6- to 8-ounce / 175 to 240ml glass with ice, pour in 1 to 2 ounces / 30 to 60ml of sage syrup, and stir. Pour the pineapple mixture into the glass to about three-quarters full, stir, and top with sparkling water (if using). Garnish with fresh sage leaves.

For goddess-like bubbles (second fermentation): Once the pineapple mixture is at the desired fermentation, fill 6- to 8-ounce / 175 to 240ml fermentation-safe bottles one-quarter full with Sage Simple Syrup and top with fermented pineapple juice, leaving about an inch of space in the bottle. Cork and place upright in a dry, dark place for 7 to 8 days, uncorking for a few seconds between the second and third days, so that bubbles can form.

Schlond's Embrace

As the Grumpy Lily in Deastok serves it, Schlond's Embrace begins by distilling and fermenting mint over a period of forty years. The gods bless those alcohol makers; we simply do not have that kind of patience. Nor, we realized after sampling the original drink, do we have that kind of stomach. So, deciding that discretion is the better part of valor, we have created a nonalcoholic version of the Embrace that honors its flavor profile without the same gut punch to the innards. For those who miss the overt, mushroomy tones of the alcoholic version or just want a little extra fun in their toppings, we've included a chopped shiitake garnish.

PREP TIME: 1 hour 10 minutes
COOK TIME: 5 minutes

───

⅓ cup / 65g granulated sugar

⅓ cup / 80ml water

¼ cup / 20g unsweetened cocoa powder, plus more for dusting

1 cup / 12g fresh mint leaves, lightly packed, plus 4 small mint sprigs, for garnish

2 to 3 tablespoons chaga mushroom powder

¼ teaspoon ground cinnamon, plus more for dusting

2 cups / 475ml plain nondairy milk (such as oat, almond, soy)

3 cups / 450g ice cubes

2 teaspoons chopped sliced dried shiitake mushrooms (optional)

In a small saucepan over medium heat, whisk together the sugar, water, and cocoa powder. Cook, whisking frequently, until the sugar and cocoa are completely dissolved and the mixture starts to lightly bubble around the side of the saucepan, 3 to 5 minutes. Turn off the heat, add the mint leaves, and stir until completely wilted. Cool the chocolate-mint syrup completely at room temperature, at least 1 hour.

Strain the chocolate-mint syrup into a blender. Using the back of a wooden spoon or spatula, press down on the mint to extract every last drop of the syrup, and discard the mint. Add the chaga powder and cinnamon and blend until thoroughly combined and smooth, about 1 minute—you want to dissolve the chaga powder as much as possible. Add the milk and blend again until very well combined and smooth, with no visible streaks of the syrup in the milk. Add the ice and blend until smooth. Divide the blended "chagaccino" among four short drinking glasses and garnish each drink with a mint sprig, a sprinkle of chopped shiitake mushrooms (if using), and a light dusting of additional cocoa powder and cinnamon. Serve immediately.

Athodan's Mistake

Many mysterious artifacts have made their way south from Aeor, the pre-Calamity floating city that now lies in ruins amid the ice of Eiselcross. Odd power sources, strange automata, descriptions of lost magic: these types of relics are squirreled away for study or sold for a fortune. But sometimes treasure takes other forms. This recipe—found jotted alongside far more confidential lab notes—concerns a researcher named Athodan. Apparently one of his early experiments involved, as best as we can tell, directing some kind of gravity magic into a batch of overripe fruit to reverse the fruit's aging process. It may have worked; it was hard to tell, since the fruit was liquefied and tossed all over the room. The mixture proved to be surprisingly tasty, and recreations of the drink were used to both taunt and celebrate Athodan at various festivities in the following months.

PREP TIME: 5 minutes
___

4 ounces / 120ml coconut milk

4 ounces / 120ml pineapple juice

4 ounces / 120ml white rum

2 ounces / 60ml cream of coconut (see Note)

1 ounce / 30ml fresh lime juice (from about 1 lime)

3 cups / 400g ice cubes

2 ounces / 60ml blue curaçao

Add the coconut milk, pineapple juice, rum, cream of coconut, lime juice, and ice to a blender. Blend on high speed, stopping and scraping down the sides of the blender as needed, until the ice is completely broken down and the drink is smooth and thick.

Divide the drink between two chilled 16-ounce / 475ml glasses. Top each glass with 1 ounce / 30ml of the blue curaçao and serve immediately.

NOTE: Cream of coconut (not to be confused with coconut cream) is a thick, sweetened coconut syrup used primarily to make cocktails. It can be found in a can or squeeze bottle in the mixers section of most grocery stores or liquor stores.

Popping Hot Chocolate Bombs

When you want to cheer someone up, what do you give them? Are you like Caduceus, giving out little chocolate balls that, when dropped into a cup of hot water, turn into hot chocolate? Or are you more like Beau, giving out firecrackers? Wait, don't answer, it's a trick question: Now you can be both! These magical creations start like regular hot chocolate balls: a chocolate shell with homemade cocoa powder and mini marshmallows hidden in the center. But ours have fizzy candy packed inside, so they crackle and sizzle delightfully before settling down into a soothing and delicious treat.

PREP TIME: 45 minutes
COOK TIME: 10 minutes
SPECIAL EQUIPMENT: One instant-read thermometer, two 6-cavity silicone half-sphere molds (each cavity 2½ inches / 6.5cm wide), powder-free latex gloves (optional)

———

⅓ cup / 25g unsweetened cocoa powder

⅓ cup / 65g packed light brown sugar

⅛ teaspoon fine sea salt

12 ounces / 340g high-quality bittersweet chocolate, finely chopped

4½ tablespoons / 50g miniature semisweet chocolate chips

¾ cup / 35g miniature marshmallows

1½ tablespoons multicolored popping candies, such as Pop Rocks

Rainbow sparkling sugar, for sprinkling

7½ to 9 cups / 1.8 to 2.1L milk

Place two 6-cavity silicone half-sphere molds on a large baking sheet and set aside. In a medium bowl, whisk together the cocoa powder, brown sugar, and sea salt and set this hot cocoa mixture aside.

Set out a large metal or glass bowl that fits snugly on top of a medium or large saucepan. Put 8 ounces / 225g of the chopped bittersweet chocolate into the bowl. Fill the saucepan with ½ inch of water, bring to a simmer over medium heat, then immediately reduce the heat to low. Place the bowl with the chopped chocolate on top of the saucepan and stir the chocolate frequently until it is mostly melted (a few unmelted pieces are fine) and the temperature reaches 110°F / 43°C on an instant-read thermometer, about 3 minutes. Turn off the heat and remove the bowl from the saucepan (reserve the saucepan and water to use later to remelt the chocolate for topping the hot chocolate bombs). Carefully wipe any water off the bottom of the bowl. Place the bowl on a dry kitchen towel or trivet and cool the chocolate down to 100°F / 38°C, stirring occasionally. Once the melted chocolate is at temperature, add the remaining 4 ounces / 115g of chopped bittersweet chocolate in 2 or 3 additions, stirring well after each addition. Continue stirring until the chocolate is completely melted. The tempered chocolate should be smooth, thick, and glossy, with an internal temperature of around 90°F / 32°C (see Note).

recipe continues ☛

Scoop a heaping tablespoon of the tempered chocolate into one cavity of a silicone mold. Use a dry pastry brush to brush the chocolate evenly on the bottom and up the sides and inner edges of the cavity. The chocolate should be thick and coat the inside evenly. If any chocolate pools at the bottom of the mold, remove it with a spoon or the back of the pastry brush and return the excess chocolate to the bowl of tempered chocolate. Repeat until all of the cavities are coated with chocolate. Cover the bowl with the remaining tempered chocolate with plastic wrap and set aside. Let the chocolate in the molds sit at room temperature until the chocolate turns from shiny to matte and is mostly set, 20 to 30 minutes. Transfer the molds to the refrigerator and chill until the chocolate is completely set and hardened, 5 to 10 additional minutes.

Wearing powder-free latex gloves (if desired), gently remove the chocolate half-spheres from the molds and transfer, open sides up, to a 12-cup muffin pan. This makes filling the bombs so much easier. Divide the hot cocoa mixture evenly among six of the half-spheres and top evenly with the miniature semisweet chocolate chips, miniature marshmallows, and popping candies.

Warm a small nonstick skillet over very low heat. Working quickly, set an unfilled half-sphere on the skillet, open side down, for just a second to warm the chocolate (use a spoon to lift each half-sphere out of the muffin cup if needed). Set it, open side down, on top of a filled half-sphere, matching the seams as much as possible. If needed, you can use your fingers to help seal the edges of the sphere.

Repeat with the remaining half-spheres to make 5 additional bombs. Let sit at room temperature until set and completely hardened, 10 to 15 minutes.

Meanwhile, bring the water in the saucepan back to a bare simmer and reheat the reserved tempered chocolate until it is just melted, around 2 minutes, stirring frequently. The temperature of the chocolate should get no higher than 90°F / 32°C, to keep the chocolate tempered. Turn off the heat, remove the bowl from the saucepan, and carefully wipe any water off the bottom of the bowl. Place the bowl on a dry kitchen towel or trivet. The chocolate should be warm and fluid but not hot to the touch. Transfer the chocolate to a small plastic storage bag and cut a very small opening in one corner of the bag.

Drizzle the chocolate on top of the hot chocolate bombs and immediately sprinkle with rainbow sparkling sugar. Let the bombs sit again until the drizzled chocolate is hardened and set, 10 to 15 minutes.

To serve, heat 1¼ to 1½ cups / 300 to 360ml of milk per bomb until very hot and steamy (the amount of milk will depend on the size of the mugs you are using). Add the bombs to six large mugs, then carefully pour the hot milk over the hot chocolate bombs and STAND BACK! The hot chocolate bombs will melt, and the popping candies will start to pop, sizzle, and sputter. Once the popping stops, give the cocoa a good stir and enjoy.

NOTE: If you want to skip the step of tempering the chocolate, you can use 12 ounces / 340g good-quality dark chocolate–flavored melting wafers instead. Avoid using candy melts; those tend to not have a strong chocolate flavor, so your hot chocolate will be less tasty.

Popping Malted Hot Cocoa Mix
(an alternative for the beginning adventurer!)

PREP TIME: 10 minutes

½ cup / 100g packed light brown sugar

½ cup / 60g confectioners' sugar

½ cup / 40g unsweetened cocoa powder

½ cup / 45g dry whole or nonfat milk powder

½ cup / 55g malted milk powder

1 teaspoon cornstarch

½ teaspoon fine sea salt

One 4-ounce / 115g bar high-quality bittersweet chocolate

1½ cups / 75g miniature marshmallows

2 teaspoons multicolored popping candies, such as Pop Rocks, plus more for garnish

Water or milk, for serving

Whipped cream, for topping

Set a fine-mesh strainer over a medium bowl, then spoon the brown sugar, confectioners' sugar, cocoa powder, milk powder, malted milk powder, cornstarch, and fine sea salt into the strainer. Use a rubber spatula or a large spoon to stir and push the dry ingredients through the strainer. Whisk the strained ingredients until the mixture is completely combined, with no lumps left behind. Set the hot cocoa mix aside.

Place the bar of bittersweet chocolate in a resealable plastic storage bag and use a rolling pin, the smooth side of a meat mallet, or the back of a heavy skillet to break the chocolate into smaller pieces and shards. Transfer the broken-up chocolate to the bowl with the hot cocoa mix along with the miniature marshmallows and multicolored popping candies. Stir to combine.

For each serving, heat 1½ cups / 360ml of water or milk until very hot and steamy. Place ⅓ cup / 41g of the hot cocoa mix in the bottom of a large mug (see Note), then carefully add the hot water or milk. Stir until the hot cocoa is smooth and creamy. Be cautious here, because the popping candies will pop, sizzle, and sputter as the water or milk is added to the cocoa mix. Top the hot cocoa with whipped cream, garnish with a very light sprinkle of additional popping candies, and serve immediately.

NOTE: For an extra chocolaty hot cocoa, use ½ cup / 61.5g of the mix per serving. Transfer any leftover hot cocoa mix into an airtight container and store at room temperature for up to 3 months.

Dead People Tea

We've already discussed how important the cycle of life and death is to Caduceus, including his hobby of cooking with plants grown from corpses.* Tea is also extremely important to Caduceus. When the rest of the Mighty Nein met him, he offered them tea before he offered his name or learned theirs. And yes, that tea was made from dead people.** It was also very tasty. If you've never made your own tea, from whatever source, we highly recommend trying it. Why not start with this gorgeous mix? The bulk of the drying can be done in the oven overnight, the tea stays good for up to six months, and the brewed color evokes those red-purple flowers that Caduceus first served the Mighty Nein.***

*See Caduceus's Ethically Sourced Mushroom Toasts (page 185).

**Again we point out, as Caduceus would: Aren't most things?

***From the Casala family, Caduceus would like us to remind you. Once they made textiles. Now they make excellent tea.

PREP TIME: 1 hour 15 minutes
TOTAL TIME: 8 hours 15 minutes
SPECIAL EQUIPMENT: Four "junior" coffee filters (small size) and kitchen twine

---

One 1½-inch / 4cm piece ginger root

3 small branches fresh thyme (3 or 4 stems each)

2 cups / 24g fresh mint leaves, lightly packed

1 cup / 12g fresh lemon balm leaves, lightly packed (see Notes)

½ cup / 25g dried hibiscus flowers, lightly packed

Honey, for serving

Position two racks in the upper-middle and lower-middle of the oven and preheat to 175°F / 80°C. Line two baking sheets with parchment paper and set aside.

Peel the ginger and use a very sharp knife or a kitchen mandolin to very thinly cut the ginger crosswise into paper-thin slices. Lay the thyme branches in one corner of one of the prepared baking sheets, then spread the ginger slices in a single layer around the rest of the baking sheet. Spread the mint and lemon balm leaves in a single layer on the second prepared baking sheet.

Place the baking sheet with the thyme and ginger on the lower rack of the oven and bake until both are very dry and brittle, about 1 hour. After 30 minutes, start opening the oven door to check on the thyme and ginger. If you notice either starting to brown at all before they are dry, crack the oven door open slightly to release some heat.

recipe continues ☞

Once the thyme and ginger are dry, immediately turn off the heat to the oven and place the baking sheet with the mint and lemon balm leaves on the upper rack. Leave the ginger and herbs in the oven until the mint and lemon balm leaves also dry out and become brittle, 8 to 12 hours. The timing for this will depend heavily on the residual heat of the oven and the moisture in the herbs and ginger.

Pick the thyme leaves off of the woody branches and transfer the leaves to a medium bowl along with the dried mint and lemon balm leaves, sliced ginger, and hibiscus flowers. Stir to combine.

Divide the dried tea mix into four equal portions. Place one portion in the center of a "junior" coffee filter, then completely enclose the tea mix by gathering the filter at the top and tying the top together using kitchen twine. Repeat this with the remaining tea mix and coffee filters to make four large "tea bags." If you have a teapot with an infuser, you can skip this step and just use a quarter of the dried tea mix for every 4 cups / 950ml of boiling water your teapot holds.

To make one pot of tea, add 1 large tea bag to a large teapot and pour 4 cups / 950ml of boiling water into the teapot. Let the tea steep for 5 minutes. Pour the hot tea into teacups and serve immediately with honey on the side.

NOTES: If you cannot find fresh lemon balm, you can substitute extra mint leaves instead.

Place any leftover tea mix in an airtight container and store in a cool, dark area of your kitchen for up to 6 months.

Acknowledgments

We would like to thank the cast of *Critical Role*—Matthew Mercer, Taliesin Jaffe, Marisha Ray, Travis Willingham, Laura Bailey, Ashley Johnson, Sam Riegel, and Liam O'Brien— for creating this fantastic world, and a special thank you to Dani Carr, Shaunette DeTie, Niki Chi, and the rest of the *Critical Role* team. And thanks also to Sarah Malarkey, Sarah Peed, Lydia Estrada, Ashley Pierce, Ian Dingman, Heather Williamson, and the entire Penguin Random House crew.

Also, Liz would like to thank the Critical Role Wiki and CritRoleStats for their devotion and thoroughness, Nachie Marsham for the constant encouragement, and Jessica Jackson for the fastest puns in the realm.

Jesse would like to thank Dennis Green for being an expert taste tester, Susan Vu for helping talk through recipes, and Jena Szewczyk for helping come up with several of the most nerdy and genius concepts he has developed.

Susan would like to thank the *Critical Role* team for reminding us human folks that it is okay (and a lot of fun!) to play make believe well after childhood. Thank you also to Liz, Sarah Malarkey, Sarah Peed, and my two amazing co-recipe developers for making this process delightfully whimsical and delicious.

Amanda would like to thank her nieces Storm and River and nephew Mozes for making play, laughter, silliness, curiosity, and imagination a part of daily living. I love you, crazy noodles. Thank you to my agent, Danielle Svetcov—you always go above and beyond—and the Michael Jordan to my Scottie Pippen, Bryant Terry. You's my gee.

Index